"This is an outstanding book that I look forward to using in teaching. It is ideally suited to a political philosophy or philosophy of law class. The writing is very accessible and the arguments sharply focussed. As in any good debate, one finds oneself changing one's mind, after reading each chapter! The authors do an excellent job, and I recommend this book enthusiastically."

John Martin Fischer, *University of California, Riverside*

Is Political Authority an Illusion?

What gives some people the right to issue commands to everyone else and force everyone else to obey them? And why should people obey the commands of those with political power? These two key questions are the heart of the issue of political authority, and, in this book, two philosophers debate the answers.

Michael Huemer argues that political authority is an illusion and that no one is entitled to rule over anyone. He discusses and rebuts the major theories supporting political authority: implicit social contract theory, hypothetical contract theories, democratic theories of authority, and utilitarian theories. Daniel Layman argues that democratic governments have authority because they are needed to protect our rights and because they are accountable to the people. Each author writes two replies directly addressing the arguments and ideas of the other.

Key Features

- Covers a key foundational problem of political philosophy: the authority of government
- Debate format ensures a full hearing of both sides
- A Glossary includes key concepts in political philosophy related to the issue of authority
- Annotated Further Reading sections point students to additional resources
- Clear, concrete examples and arguments help students clearly see both sides of the argument
- A Foreword by Matt Zwolinski describes a broader context for political authority and then traces the key points and turns in the authors' debate

Michael Huemer is Professor of Philosophy at the University of Colorado at Boulder, USA. He is the author of more than 70 academic articles in ethics, epistemology, political philosophy, and metaphysics, as well as seven amazing books that you should immediately buy, including *The Problem of Political Authority* (2013), *Dialogues on Ethical Vegetarianism* (2019), and *Justice Before the Law* (2021).

Daniel Layman is Associate Professor of Philosophy at Davidson College, USA and specializes in political theory and the history of political thought. He is the author of numerous articles in leading journals and the book, *Locke Among the Radicals: Liberty and Property in the Nineteenth Century* (2020).

Matt Zwolinski is Professor of Philosophy and Director of the Center for Ethics, Economics, and Public Policy at the University of San Diego, USA.

Little Debates About Big Questions

About the series:

Philosophy asks questions about the fundamental nature of reality, our place in the world, and what we should do. Some of these questions are perennial: for example, *Do we have free will? What is morality?* Some are much newer: for example, *How far should free speech on campus extend? Are race, sex and gender social constructs?* But all of these are among the big questions in philosophy and they remain controversial.

Each book in the *Little Debates About Big Questions* series features two professors on opposite sides of a big question. Each author presents their own side, and the authors then exchange objections and replies. Short, lively, and accessible, these debates showcase diverse and deep answers. Pedagogical features include standard form arguments, section summaries, bolded key terms and principles, glossaries, and annotated reading lists.

The debate format is an ideal way to learn about controversial topics. Whereas the usual essay or book risks overlooking objections against its own thesis or misrepresenting the opposite side, in a debate each side can make their case at equal length, and then present objections the other side must consider. Debates have a more conversational and fun style too, and we selected particularly talented philosophers – in substance and style – for these kinds of encounters.

Debates can be combative – sometimes even descending into anger and animosity. But debates can also be cooperative. While our authors disagree strongly, they work together to help each other and the reader get clearer on the ideas, arguments, and objections. This is intellectual progress, and a much-needed model for civil and constructive disagreement.

The substance and style of the debates will captivate interested readers new to the questions. But there's enough to interest experts too. The debates will be especially useful for courses in philosophy and related subjects – whether as primary or as secondary readings – and a few debates can be combined to make up the reading for an entire course.

We thank the authors for their help in constructing this series. We are honored to showcase their work. They are all preeminent scholars or rising stars in their fields, and through these debates they share what's been discovered with a wider audience. This is a paradigm for public philosophy and will impress upon students, scholars, and other interested readers the enduring importance of debating the big questions.

Tyron Goldschmidt, Fellow of the Rutgers Center for Philosophy of Religion, USA
Dustin Crummett, Ludwig Maximilian University of Munich, Germany

Published Titles:

Is Political Authority an Illusion?: A Debate
by Michael Huemer and Daniel Layman

Selected Forthcoming Titles:

Should We Want to Live Forever?: A Debate
by Stephen Cave and John Martin Fischer

Do Numbers Exist?: A Debate
by William Lane Craig and Peter van Inwagen

What Do We Owe Other Animals?: A Debate
by Bob Fischer and Anja Jauernig

What Does Evolution Mean for Morality?: A Debate
by Helen De Cruz and Johan De Smedt

What is Consciousness?: A Debate
by Amy Kind and Daniel Stoljar

Consequentialism or Virtue Ethics?: A Debate
by Jorge L.A. Garcia and Alastair Norcross

Are We Made of Matter?: A Debate
by Eric T. Olson and Aaron Segal

For more information about this series, please visit: www.routledge.com/Little-Debates-about-Big-Questions/book-series/LDABQ

Is Political Authority an Illusion?

A Debate

Michael Huemer and Daniel Layman

With a Foreword by Matt Zwolinski

Routledge
Taylor & Francis Group
NEW YORK AND LONDON

First published 2022
by Routledge
605 Third Avenue, New York, NY 10158

and by Routledge
2 Park Square, Milton Park, Abingdon, Oxon, OX14 4RN

Routledge is an imprint of the Taylor & Francis Group, an informa business

© 2022 Taylor & Francis

Library of Congress Cataloging-in-Publication Data
A catalog record for this book has been requested

ISBN: 978-0-367-45774-7 (hbk)
ISBN: 978-0-367-34745-1 (pbk)
ISBN: 978-0-429-32804-6 (ebk)

DOI: 10.4324/9780429328046

Typeset in Sabon
by Apex CoVantage, LLC

Contents

Foreword

Do Governments Have Political Authority?

Matt Zwolinski

When you stop to think about it, governments are pretty strange creatures. After all, governments claim for themselves the right to do lots of things that nobody else can do. Governments can take your money without your consent, and this is called "taxation" rather than "robbery." Governments can forcibly seize you and lock you in a cage for violating its rules, and this is called "arrest and imprisonment" rather than "kidnapping." Governments can tell you what foods and medicines you are allowed to consume, and this is called "regulation" rather than "being a busybody."

What gives governments the right to do these things? Or is it possible that governments actually *don't* have the right to do these things? After all, governments in the past have claimed lots of rights that we now think they didn't really have: the right to enforce slavery, the right to deny suffrage to women and propertyless men, and the right to engage in colonial conquest in foreign lands. If governments in the past were mistaken to claim these rights, maybe our governments are mistaken about some of the rights they claim, too. Maybe, in fact, they're mistaken about virtually *all* of the rights they claim.

Political philosophers have been thinking about issues like these for centuries. And with good reason! Government pervades almost every aspect of our lives – from how we can earn a living, to whom we can marry, to what sort of medical care we can seek (and afford). Its policies can have a deep and profound impact on our individual lives and on the shape of the societies in which we live. If it turns out that governments actually *don't* have many of the rights that they claim, that's more than just a theoretically interesting conclusion. That's a conclusion that ought to radically change the way people live their lives.

DOI: 10.4324/9780429328046-1

And, of course, that conclusion actually *has* changed not only the lives of numerous individuals but also the entire course of history. The American Revolution was based on the Jeffersonian idea that governments are bound to respect people's natural rights to "life, liberty, and the pursuit of happiness," and that "whenever any form of government becomes destructive of these ends, it is the right of the people to alter or abolish it." In these famous lines from the Declaration of Independence, Jefferson is making a philosophical claim about the nature of government's rights – an idea he got from John Locke. A little over a decade later in France, another revolution was launched based largely on the philosophical ideas of Rousseau. And a little over a century after that, yet another revolution occurred in Russia, this time drawing heavily on the ideas of Karl Marx. Surely, the economist John Maynard Keynes was correct when he wrote in the twentieth century that "the ideas of economists and political philosophers, both when they are right and when they are wrong, are more powerful than is commonly understood. Indeed, the world is ruled by little else. Practical men, who believe themselves to be quite exempt from any intellectual influences, are usually slaves of some defunct economist."[1] Or philosopher!

If you're intrigued by these questions about the nature and limits of political authority and you want to think about them in a more careful and systematic way, then you've opened the right book. This book does exactly the kind of thing that made me fall in love with philosophy when I was in college. It takes a big, perennially important question about the human condition and tries to make sense of it through clear, rigorous reasoning. By the time you've finished it, you might not have a final, settled answer to all of the questions about political authority. But you'll have a much better understanding of what those questions are and what some of the key issues and arguments are that you'll need to keep in mind in exploring them further.

For example, one way that we can start to get clearer about the issue is to notice that questions about the role of government have two different, but related, aspects. One issue is whether governments have any rights to be making laws and ordering people

---

1. Keynes 1997.

around at all. Philosophers call this the question of *political legitimacy*. A government is legitimate if it has the right to rule; illegitimate if it does not. A different issue is what *duties* citizens have with respect to the laws their government makes. Do you have an obligation to do what your government tells you to do, just because it tells you so? This is the question of *political obligation*. If we put political legitimacy and political obligation together, we get *political authority*. A government has political authority if it is legitimate and if its citizens have political obligation.

Let's start by thinking a bit more carefully about how these two ideas are related. Suppose you think that the government under which you live is generally legitimate, but that in the case of some particular laws, it exceeds the bounds of its legitimacy. So, for instance, you might think that the U.S. government is perfectly justified in enforcing traffic laws, running a post office, and regulating CO_2 emissions and a host of other things, but that it has no right to criminalize the possession and use of marijuana. In this case, you face a difficult question regarding political obligation. Are you obligated to obey *all* of the government's laws, including the ones you think are unjust? Or should you conclude with St. Augustine that *lex iniustia non est lex* – an unjust law is no law at all – and that you therefore have no moral obligation to refrain from smoking marijuana just because the government says so?

The existence of unjust laws poses a challenge for political authority and raises a host of difficult and interesting philosophical questions. What if a government has not merely one unjust law but many? At what point does the existence of such unjust laws undermine the government's claim to legitimacy? And what methods, exactly, may citizens use in resisting unjust laws? Are they required to disobey publicly and to accept whatever consequences the state imposes upon them for their civil disobedience? Or may they disobey secretly and try to avoid the punishment? At what point are individuals permitted to use violence to resist the enforcement of unjust laws? At what point are they permitted to revolt against the state?

This book will devote some attention to these questions, and as you will see, Michael Huemer and Daniel Layman will take very different approaches to answering them. For the most part, however, this book is devoted to an even more fundamental question. Rather than focusing on how the existence of unjust laws affects political authority, this book asks whether political authority even exists *at all*. Is political authority even possible? Is it simply an illusion?

Such a radical thought will no doubt conjure the specter of anarchism in the mind of some readers. And, indeed, the claim that political authority is an illusion *is* a sort of anarchism. But it is important in this context to distinguish between two somewhat different senses the term "anarchism" can have. One sort of anarchism denies the existence of political obligation and thereby holds that individuals do not have a general obligation to obey the law. This is usually called *philosophical anarchism*. Philosophical anarchism is often contrasted with *political anarchism*, a doctrine which holds that governments ought to be abolished and that it would be better (more beneficial or more just) for human beings to live together in a stateless society.

When most people think of anarchism, they're really thinking of *political* anarchism. And, indeed, many of history's most famous anarchists have been political anarchists. The Frenchman Pierre Joseph Proudhon and the Russians Mikhail Bakunin and Peter Kropotkin, for example, not only thought that a stateless society would be a good thing, but they also actively devoted a good portion of their lives toward the pursuit of that goal. Some political anarchists have pursued their goal through peaceful argument and propaganda. Others, notoriously, have pursued it through violence and terrorism.

But it's possible to be a philosophical anarchist without being a political anarchist. It's possible, in other words, to think that one has no moral duty to obey the law as such without believing that government should be abolished altogether. Indeed, it's possible to think that one has no moral *obligation* to obey the law without believing that one *should* disobey the law, all things considered. A philosophical anarchist might think that the government has no authority to tell him not to smoke marijuana, but that it's nevertheless a good idea not to smoke marijuana. Perhaps because it's unhealthy, or perhaps simply because she recognizes that the state has a lot of *power* and so, whether it has authority or not, it's generally a good idea to do what it says out of sheer *prudence*. Philosophical anarchists thus need not be bomb throwers. Your best friend might be a philosophical anarchist without you even knowing it. You might even be one yourself.

In his opening essay, Michael Huemer argues for a form of philosophical anarchism. In doing so, he draws on an idea that has played an important role in the history of political philosophy, which others have called the "moral parity thesis."[2] The basic idea of the moral parity thesis is that governments and their agents have no rights that are not identical to or derivable from the rights of ordinary individuals. In other words, all people – whether private actors or government agents – have the same basic (nonderivative) rights and duties, such that whatever is wrong for private citizens to do is (generally) wrong for an agent of the government to do as well.

Stated as such, the moral parity thesis sounds unassuming, even trivial. But as Huemer demonstrates, its political implications are radical. If it is wrong for individuals to take others' money without consent, then it is wrong for governments to do it, too. If it would be wrong for your neighbor to coercively prevent you from eating food he/she deems unhealthy, it is wrong for the government to do it, too. According to the moral parity thesis, governments have *no* rights that ordinary citizens don't have. But if that's true, then what's left of the idea of political authority? The logical implication of moral parity seems to be philosophical anarchism.

We can find something like the moral parity thesis in John Locke's *Second Treatise of Government*. Locke claimed that when someone violates another's rights, "the injury and the crime is equal, whether committed by the wearer of a crown, or some petty villain."[3] In other words, just because it's a government taking your money without your consent rather than a common thief, that doesn't make it any less a robbery. Theft is theft, no matter how many people are involved in perpetrating it, and no matter what official titles they might bear.

Of course, Locke didn't think that taxation was robbery. Locke believed in moral parity, but he was no anarchist. That's because Locke thought that government derived its special powers (like the power to tax) from the consent of the governed. Individuals have natural rights to freedom and property, but they can choose to give government the right to impose taxes and restrictions on them via a

---

2. See Brennan 2021, p. 236. Brennan describes the moral parity thesis as holding that "government agents and private civilians are fundamentally morally equal." The formulation above is taken from Zwolinski and Tomasi 2022, chapter 1. Layman attributes to Huemer a similar, but somewhat different principle which he calls "Anti-Exceptionalism."

3. Locke 1952, §176.

social contract. It's like buying a house that's governed by a Home-owners Association (HOA). The HOA has the right to charge you dues and limit what colors you paint your house, but that's only because you *gave* it those rights when you signed the contract. For Huemer, though, this strategy doesn't work. Political authority can't be justified by a social contract because, as the nineteenth-century American anarchist Lysander Spooner argued, there simply never *was* any social contract.[4] Neither the U.S. government nor any other government in the history of the world obtained its power through the unanimous consent of its citizens. And even if the U.S. government *had* been founded that way, the contract would only have bound the people who actually signed it. People like you and me aren't morally obligated by promises our ancestors made hundreds of years in the past.

Some philosophers try to get around this inconvenient fact by arguing that people *tacitly* consent to government. In other words, you might not have actually signed a contract, but you live here, or you vote, or you pay taxes. And by engaging in those activities, you're *implicitly* consenting to government's authority. But Hue-mer doesn't think that this sort of argument works either. As the philosopher Robert Nozick quipped, "tacit consent isn't worth the paper it's not written on."[5] To note just one problem with the theory, it doesn't seem reasonable to assume that a philosophical anarchist like Huemer is *tacitly* consenting to government by pay-ing his taxes when he is *explicitly* writing a series of books and articles all of which state very clearly that he does *not* consent. In any other context, explicit dissent would trump alleged tacit con-sent. The reason government nevertheless views Huemer as subject to its authority is simply that it doesn't think his consent *matters*, one way or the other.

So Huemer thinks that consent could, in principle, justify politi-cal authority. It's just that since no state in the history of the world has actually received the consent of its citizenry, this justification is purely hypothetical and doesn't do anything to ground the political authority of any actually existing regimes.

---

4. Spooner 1870.
5. Nozick 1974, p. 287.

Daniel Layman, in contrast, thinks that many (but not all) states have authority, at least to a very considerable degree. But not because people *consented* to them. The Lockean notion of consent doesn't play much role at all in Layman's argument. Instead, Layman draws primarily on the Kantian idea of individuals relating to each other as equal bearers of rights.

How does this Kantian idea help establish a justification for political authority? Well, imagine what things would be like if we didn't have a state – if we lived in a "state of nature." Thomas Hobbes famously thought that the state of nature would be a "war of all against all" and that the life of an individual in such a state would be "solitary, poor, nasty, brutish, and short."[6] In such a state, the weak would be at the mercy of the strong, the individual at the mercy of the mob – hardly the kind of situation that enables individuals to relate to each other as equal bearers of rights.

Locke had a more optimistic reading of what the state of nature would be like. But even Locke thought that individuals' rights would be threatened in the state of nature by deliberate wrongdoing and by the absence of reliable mechanisms to create, adjudicate, and enforce the kind of rules that allow people to live together peacefully. Even if your rights weren't actually violated in a situation like this, that would largely be a matter of luck. Your rights would still be subject to violation pretty much anytime somebody else felt like violating them. Though free in a sense, individuals would still be subject to having their rights violated at the arbitrary discretion of others. And if that's freedom at all, it's not the kind of freedom that people concerned to live among each other as equals should care about.

For Layman, this state of being subject to others' arbitrary will (a state which he calls "rights vitiation") is the key to understanding why we should reject the state of nature and embrace the idea of political authority. The purpose of government, for Layman, as for Locke and Kant, is to protect our rights. Hobbes thought that too, in a way. But the Hobbesian solution of an all-powerful monarch won't work for Layman even if such a government were 100% successful in preventing people's rights from being violated. The reason that it won't work is that under such a government, people would

---

6. Hobbes 1996, Chapter XIII.

still be subject to the arbitrary will of others. Only now it would be the absolute monarch, rather than their fellow citizens, to whose will they would be subject.

How can we avoid this problem? How can we establish government without making some people subject to others' arbitrary will? For Layman, the answer lies in mechanisms that render the government *accountable* to its citizens. Democracies are unlike monarchies because in a democracy, the government can't simply treat citizens any way it wants. In a democracy, government is answerable to the people. Citizens have legal standing to assert their rights against government, and there are institutional mechanisms such as elections and courts to which citizens can appeal in support of their claims. Accountable, democratic governance protects individuals' status as equals – not only against their fellow citizens, but also against government itself.

The notion of accountability thus plays a crucial role in Layman's argument and is essential for understanding many of the disagreements between him and Huemer throughout this book. Take, for instance, the issue of "anarcho-capitalism." Huemer, as it turns out, isn't merely a philosophical anarchist who thinks that individuals may permissibly disobey governments' laws. He actually goes further and thinks that it would be better if governments were abolished altogether and if the police and judicial services they currently provide were provided by private firms in the free market instead. Drawing on the tradition of Gustave de Molinari and Murray Rothbard, Huemer thinks that a purely voluntary system of competing defense agencies could solve the problems of the state of nature identified by Hobbes and Locke in a way that is both economically efficient and consistent with respect for individual rights.[7] Defensive agencies would be accountable to their clients for just the same reason that companies like Costco are accountable to their customers – they want to make a profit, and the only way to do so is to provide a quality product at an affordable price.

Layman, in contrast, argues that it is "conceptually impossible for people to live together as free and equal rights-holders under anarcho-capitalism." And the reason comes down to accountability. It's true that private defensive firms would be accountable

---

7. Molinari 1849; Rothbard 1973.

to their customers. But unlike a democratic government, which is accountable to *everyone*, a system of private defensive firms is accountable only to the highest bidder. Under such a system, the protection of individuals' rights is subject to the whims of private economic power. Just as in a Hobbesian system where the weak are at the mercy of the strong, so under anarcho-capitalism the poor would be at the mercy of the rich.

There's a lot more to be said about this issue, as there is about so many other issues covered in this book. But by now I hope I've said enough to give you a taste for what's to come. This book gives you a window onto a conversation by two incredible philosophers about an issue of immense practical and philosophical importance. It's a pleasure to read, but also a challenge. Here are two *very* different views about the nature of political authority. Which one – if either! – gets it right?

References

Brennan, Jason. 2021. "Moral Parity Between State and Non-state Actors", in *The Routledge Handbook of Anarchy and Anarchist Thought*, ed. G. Chartier and C. Van Schoelandt. London: Routledge.

Hobbes, Thomas. 1996. *Leviathan*. Cambridge: Cambridge University Press.

Keynes, John Maynard. 1997. *The General Theory of Employment, Interest, and Money*. Buffalo, NY: Prometheus Books.

Locke, John. 1952. *The Second Treatise of Government*. New York: MacMillan.

Molinari, Gustave de. 1849. "Dé la production de la sécurité", *Journal Des Économistes* 21 (1).

Nozick, Robert. 1974. *Anarchy, State, and Utopia*. New York: Basic Books.

Rothbard, Murray N. 1973. *For a New Liberty*. New York: Collier.

Spooner, Lysander. 1870. "No Treason No. VI: The Constitution of No Authority", pp. 171–229 in *The Collected Works of Lysander Spooner*, vol. 4. Indianapolis, IN: Liberty Fund.

Zwolinski, Matt and John Tomasi. 2022. *A Brief History of Libertarianism*. Princeton: Princeton University Press.

Opening Statements

Chapter 1

The Illusion of Authority

Michael Huemer

Contents

1 Introduction: The Problem of Authority

1.1 The Case of the Vigilante

In this chapter, I'm going to explain the philosophical problem of *political authority* and why some philosophers, myself included, believe that political authority is an illusion.

Let me start with a short story.[1] You and I live in a neighborhood that has a problem with vandals, who have been painting graffiti on walls, damaging property, and so on. For whatever reason, no one is doing anything about the problem (either we don't have a government or the government doesn't care). One day, I decide to do something about it. My family and I start to go around the

---

1. This story, as well as most of the ideas of this chapter, are from Huemer 2013, part 1, where all of this is discussed at much greater length.

DOI: 10.4324/9780429328046-3

neighborhood armed, looking for vandals. When we find one, we kidnap him at gunpoint and lock him in a cage in our basement, where we plan to hold the vandal captive for a few years to teach him a lesson.

After we've been doing this for a few months, crime has noticeably declined. I then decide to make the rounds of the neighborhood, collecting my fee. What, you didn't think I would perform this crucial service for *free*, did you? So I show up at your door one day, visibly armed, and I announce that your fee for my services for the last month comes to $500. Cash or credit card is accepted.

You protest that you never agreed to buy my services and, therefore, owe me nothing. You're also not sure how you feel about this whole "locking vandals in the basement" project, which strikes you as a bit insane. I reply that if you don't want my protection, you're free to sell your house and leave the neighborhood. Otherwise, payment is mandatory, as determined by me. Should you refuse to pay what you owe me, I will unfortunately have to take *you* captive, by force, and lock you in a cage in my basement along with the neighborhood's other miscreants.

Oh, and by the way, I have determined that some of the food you've been eating is unhealthy for you. You will, therefore, no longer be permitted to buy or sell certain products. I will be posting a list of unacceptable foods, beverages, and other consumer goods shortly. If you want to avoid being kidnaped at gunpoint, you'll check that list and make sure your behavior conforms to my commands.

End of story. Now I want to ask two related philosophical questions about it. Question 1: Is my behavior in this story morally acceptable? Question 2: In this story, do you have a moral obligation to obey my orders and pay me $500?

Most people have little trouble answering these questions. The answer to both is *obviously* no. Indeed, to think otherwise would strike us as crazy.

Now, just in case you haven't yet noticed, here is what is interesting about this story. What I do in that story is the same sort of thing that the government does all the time. I make rules for other people to follow (allegedly for their own good), I kidnap people who disobey me and imprison them, and I force other people to pay me for my services. These are the main activities of a government, though they use different words to describe them: "legislation," "criminal justice," and "taxation." When *I* do these things, people think I am crazy or evil and no one should obey me. When the *government* does them, we think it is necessary and good, and apart from perhaps a few special circumstances, we tend to think everyone should obey the government's commands.

That is a pretty stark difference. Can it be *justified*? In other words, is there some *morally relevant difference* between the government and me that would explain why they are entitled to do things that would be wrong for you or me to do and why we should obey them even though we would have no obligation to obey similar commands given by anyone else?

1.2 The Idea of Political Authority

The idea of **political authority** addresses the preceding questions. The reason why *my* behavior in the Vigilante story is wrong yet the *government's* behavior is okay is (allegedly) that *I don't have any authority*, but the government does. For example, I don't have the authority to tax people, but the government (allegedly) *does* have that authority.

What is meant by "authority" here? We're speaking here of a particular kind of authority, *political* authority (as opposed to, say, parental authority, or the authority of your boss, or the intellectual authority of scientists). The idea of political authority, as I define it, has two components. To have political authority, an organization must have (i) a special moral entitlement to impose its rules, by force, on the rest of society and (ii) a special capacity to generate moral obligations, in individuals, by issuing commands to them. The entitlement to forcibly impose its rules is what I call "**political legitimacy.**" The obligation to obey the commands of the state is what I call "**political obligation.**" So, in my terminology, the government has political authority if and only if (i) the government has political legitimacy *and* (ii) the citizens have political obligations to the government.

Now, I need to explain a little more what I mean by all of that. When I speak of a "special" entitlement, I mean that the entitlement only applies to that agent – in this case, *only* the government is thought to have this entitlement to forcibly impose rules on everyone else. No private individual or group is entitled to do that even if they are trying to impose the same sort of rules, by the same sort of methods, for the same purposes. Similarly, political obligation, if it exists, has the peculiar feature that it is owed only to this one agent: we are thought to be obligated to obey the commands of *the state*, where we would not be obligated to obey otherwise similar commands issued by any private individual or group.

To be clear, I am not saying that you are not obligated to obey *any* commands given by private individuals. For instance, if you are on someone else's property, you might be obligated to obey their command to leave their property. Nor am I saying that private individuals may not coercively enforce *any* rules. Again, if you are trespassing on someone's property, they may be ethically entitled to force you to leave. What I am saying that the state is thought to be entitled to issue a much *wider range* of commands, in a much wider range of circumstances, than private agents, and we are, allegedly, obligated to obey them. You don't have to be on their property, or have accepted a contract to work for them, or have any other special condition. They can just decide one day that, for example, no one in the society is allowed to buy or sell a particular product. A private individual cannot do that – that is, if a private individual tries to do that, that individual will have no entitlement to coercively enforce his or her decision, nor will the rest of us have any obligation to obey.

One aspect of the notion of authority is especially important to emphasize: the idea of authority inherently means that the agent *does not have to be objectively right*. That is to say, if A has *authority*, that means that there need not be independent moral reasons for the particular actions that A commands; the mere fact that A has commanded an action is enough to generate an obligation to perform that action even if the action was not initially obligatory or even useful. This condition is known as **content-independence;** we say that the state has a content-independent entitlement to enforce its commands, and citizens have a content-independent obligation to obey.

Consider the sort of response that parents sometimes give to children who question their commands:

Parent: Go clean your room.
Child: Why?
Parent: Because I said so.

"Because I said so" is a claim of authority: the parent claims that her merely issuing the imperative is enough to create an obligation to clean the room even if there was no independent reason to clean the room. Of course, whether that is correct is debatable. The point here is that the state makes a similar claim: that the mere existence of a law or other command from the state is enough to impose obligations on citizens even if there was no independent reason, or no sufficiently weighty reason, to do the things that those commands call for. At the same time, the state claims that its agents are morally entitled to enforce its laws and other commands even if those laws and commands are not particularly good ideas in themselves.

This "because I said so" condition is the key to what is strange about the idea of authority. If someone tells you to do something that was *already* morally obligatory – "Keep your promises!" "Respect the rights of others!" – there is nothing puzzling about why you should follow *those* directives. What is puzzling is when someone tells you to do things that you were *not* already required to do, and this allegedly imposes an obligation to do those things. For instance, when the government tells you to pay them a specific amount of money, you are, allegedly, morally obligated to pay them that specific amount, even though you would *not* be obligated to pay them anything if it were not legally required.

In some cases, the government issues commands that are *harmful* or even *unjust*, and yet, according to the doctrine of political authority, we are still bound to obey them. For instance, if the government is drafting people to fight in an unjust war, many people believe, one is obligated to fight in that war when called. That is of course controversial, but it illustrates the notion of content-independent authority.

1.3 Qualifications

To count as having "authority," it is not necessary that the state be morally entitled to make and enforce *any laws whatsoever*. There may be moral limits – perhaps the state is not entitled to make or enforce laws that are particularly awful, and particularly obviously so. Similarly, there may be moral limits that exempt us from having to obey particularly awful laws. Exactly where these limits are we need not discuss now; different thinkers will give different answers to that. What is important right now is that anyone who believes in "authority" must, by definition, think that at least *in some significant range of cases*, the state may enforce laws that are not independently, objectively justified, and citizens will be obliged to obey. That is enough to generate a puzzle: why should the state have this special moral status?

1.4 Confusions

Before moving on to discuss possible accounts of authority, I'm going to pause to address some conceptual confusions that sometimes occur. First, notice that in my terminology, as explained earlier, the word "political authority" does not mean "government." "Political authority" refers to a moral property that governments are often thought to have – one that I happen to think no one has. So please don't go around saying, "Huemer wants to get rid of political authority," or other nonsense like that. I don't want to *get rid of* political authority. That would be impossible since one cannot get rid of a thing that has never existed in the first place.

Also, please don't confuse political *power* with political *authority*. Even though there is no authority, there most certainly is power. Political power is simply the *ability* to forcibly impose one's will on the rest of society. As a matter of descriptive fact, governments have that ability. Authority, however, requires more than just power; it requires a *moral entitlement* to forcibly impose one's will on the rest of society. It is that moral entitlement that I question. In short, I think governments have mere power, not authority.

Also, please don't confuse this view with political anarchism (the view that we should abolish government), which I know some of you were about to do or have already done. If you want to hear about anarchy, you'll have to read something else.[2] This book is only about the problem of authority. The problem of political authority is not the problem of whether we should have a government. The problem of political authority is, again, the problem of whether and why the state has a special, content-independent entitlement to make and enforce rules for the rest of society and whether and why individuals have a special, content-independent obligation to obey said rules.

---

2. I recommend Friedman 1989; Rothbard 1978; and Huemer 2013, part 2. Terminological note: "Political anarchism" is what most people call "anarchism." By contrast, philosophers sometimes use the term "philosophical anarchism" to refer to the view that governments lack authority, or just the view that no one has political obligations.

Could there be a government that did not claim such authority? I see no obvious reason why there could not. It would be a government that only tried to enforce independently existing moral obligations and only expected citizens to follow independently justified principles. In fact, however, all the world's governments rely on the "Because we said so" justification for their commands as well as a good helping of "Because we have power and you do not."

2 The Social Contract Theory and Its Failures

2.1 The Theory

Most people appear to believe in political authority most of the time. Historically, most political philosophers also held this view, though in recent decades, skepticism about authority has grown and may now be the majority view.[3] What theories have been devised to account for this alleged authority?

Aside: Popular Views About Authority

It can be hard to tell what most people believe about a philosophical question. Surveys don't ask detailed philosophical questions, and most people wouldn't answer such questions anyway. Also, people may not be consistent. For instance, it appears that most people think that they are morally obligated to pay their taxes and to pay *the specific amount* required by law, regardless of whether that amount is higher or lower than it should be. At the same time, we think it's fine to violate the speed limit on a regular basis, just so we can get to our destination slightly sooner. It is difficult to reconcile these two attitudes. The first attitude suggests a content-independent obligation to obey the law, and one strong enough to require giving up thousands to millions of dollars, depending on one's income. The second attitude suggests either no political obligation or an obligation so weak as to be regularly outweighed

---

3. This is mostly due to the work of A. John Simmons (1979).

> by the trivial desire to get to one's destination a little bit ear-
> lier. This sort of thing is why I said that people only believe in
> political authority "most of the time."[4]

In this section, we address one of the most popular theories of authority, the **Social Contract Theory**. American students are often taught this theory in high school civics classes. The theory claims that the government has authority granted by a kind of contract between the people and the government: the government has agreed to provide law and order and to protect the people from foreign invasion. In return, the people have agreed to obey the government and pay taxes. So the reason why the government is entitled to coercively impose its rules on the rest of society is that the rest of society has *agreed* to have the government do that. And the reason why we are obligated to obey is that we have *agreed* to obey. Notice that this explains content-independence: when one signs a contract, one acquires an obligation to stick to the terms of that contract, and other people are entitled to enforce the contract, even if you had no *independent* reason (i.e., independent of the contract) to do the things specified in the contract, and even if the terms of the contract were ill-chosen.

There is just one fairly enormous and glaring problem with this account: it never happened. I'd be willing to bet that no one has ever handed you a contract that said "I agree to have a govern-ment" and asked you to sign it. No one presented the option to you verbally either. So how is this contract fiction supposed to justify anything?

In reply, most social contract theorists claim that the contract is "implicit," not explicit. An *explicit* contract is one that is actually stated in words, whether verbally or in print. An ***implicit* contract** is an agreement whose acceptance is somehow *implied* by one's behavior, without actually being put into words. For example, if you enter a restaurant and ask for an item on the menu, you are *implicitly* agreeing to pay for it – this is what your behavior would

---

4. Cf. George Klosko's focus group research on popular attitudes toward authority (2005, Chapter 9).

be assumed to imply, even though you do not (unless you are very weird) actually *say*, "and I will pay for it."

Okay, *what* about our behavior implies that we agree to obey the government and pay taxes? Here are four popular answers to this:

1. *Consent through silence:* Sometimes, a person indicates agreement with some arrangement merely by failing to object at an appropriate time – silence implies consent. For instance, suppose the philosophy department chair says, during a meeting, "Our next meeting will be Friday at 3:00. Any objections?" If no one says anything, then the members present could be said to have *implicitly* accepted the proposed meeting time. Similarly, perhaps most of us implicitly accept the social contract simply by failing to actively object to it.

2. *Consent through acceptance of benefits:* Another way to implicitly accept an arrangement is to voluntarily accept the benefits to which certain well-known conditions are attached. For example, if you ask for food in a restaurant and voluntarily accept that food, and if it is well known that such food generally comes with a certain monetary price, then you can be said to have implicitly accepted the obligation to pay that price. Similarly, perhaps citizens implicitly accept the social contract by voluntarily accepting benefits from the state – for instance, using government roads, schools, police, and money.

3. *Consent through participation:* A related idea is that one may implicitly accept an institution by voluntarily *participating* in it or taking up a particular role that is defined by that institution. Thus, if one voluntarily votes in elections, perhaps one thereby implicitly accepts the institution of democratic government.

4. *Consent through presence:* Finally, sometimes one can implicitly accept an arrangement simply by choosing to remain present in a particular location. Thus, suppose I announce, during a party at my house, that everyone who attends this party has to help me clean up at the end. If, after hearing that announcement, you remain at the party, you thereby implicitly take on the obligation to help me clean up. Similarly, perhaps merely by remaining present in the government's territory, citizens implicitly take on the obligation to obey the state.

2.2   The Failure of Implicit Consent

All of the earlier accounts of the implicit social contract fail. Let's discuss them briefly in turn:

1. *Consent through silence:* In order for silence to indicate consent, there must first be a meaningful opportunity to object, where objecting would actually have a chance of making a difference to what happens. Imagine modifying the department chair example as follows: the philosophy department chair says, during a meeting, "Our next meeting will be Friday at 3:00, and I don't care what any of you have to say about that. You're free to comment, but all objections will be ignored." This time, if no one says anything, that *cannot* be taken as communicating consent, since the chair made clear that objecting would make no difference. This case is more analogous to that of the government, which imposes its laws on everyone in the country, regardless of whether they object or not.

2. *Consent through acceptance of benefits:* The same point applies here. Acceptance of benefits can be taken as communicating consent to a given arrangement *only if* failing to accept the benefits would result in that arrangement *not* being imposed on one. In the case of the state, everyone knows that the same laws and the same taxes will be imposed on you regardless of whether you use government services or not. If, for example, you send your children to a private school, you will not get a refund of any portion of your tax bill; you will still have to pay exactly the same amount to support the public school system. Therefore, sending your kids to a public school does not mean that you consent to pay those taxes.

3. *Consent through participation:* Participation in an institution *may* indicate endorsement of that institution, but it need not. An individual may choose to participate in an institution simply because he knows that the institution is unavoidable. Again, the crucial question is what would happen if an individual did not participate. If you *didn't* vote in the elections, would you then *not* have to obey the laws made by whoever wins? Of course not. You will still be subject to exactly the same laws, whether you vote or not. Therefore, your voting in the elections does not imply that you agree to be subject to those laws.

4. *Consent through presence:* This is the most popular theory of implicit consent, yet also perhaps the most absurd. Return to the Vigilante case from Section 1.1. Suppose I declare that everyone in the neighborhood must pay me $500 a month because they have *agreed* to do so. The way that they made this agreement, I claim, is by living in their own houses. This would be ridiculous.

How does this case differ from the party example? In the party example, I declare that the partygoers must accept my condition (helping me clean up) in order to use *my property*. In the Vigilante case, I declare that neighbors must accept my condition (paying me $500 a month) in order to use *their own* property. I cannot unilaterally declare that you "agree" to do whatever I want as a condition on using your own property.

Which case is more like the government? The government demands that all individuals obey its laws and pay taxes, in order to be allowed to remain on *their own* land. If one does not want to be subject to the government, one has to leave one's own home. If one does not want *any* government, then one has to move to Antarctica (the only land mass on Earth that has no government). This is analogous to me, in the Vigilante case, demanding that my neighbors leave the neighborhood if they don't want to obey me and pay my fees.

Aside: Territorial Sovereignty

A defender of the social contract theory might argue that the entire country really does in some sense belong to the government. Perhaps not in the same sense that my house belongs to me – the country isn't literally the government's *property* – but the government has some sort of rights of control over the territory (sometimes called "territorial sovereignty"). But notice that the notion of *sovereignty* is very close to the notion of *authority*, so there is reason to worry that this reply is a form of circular reasoning. If we *don't* assume that the government already has authority, then how would we defend the claim of territorial sovereignty? The government could of course make a *law* saying that it has territorial sovereignty – but this would have no moral effect unless we assume that the government already has authority. Moreover, if we could somehow account for the government's "sovereignty," it seems very likely that *that* account, whatever it was, would be the real account of the government's authority, and thus there would be no need for the social contract theory.

2.3   Some Principles for Valid Contracts

Real contracts, as understood both in common-sense morality and in the law, satisfy certain general principles that I have implicitly made use of in the preceding discussion. The following three principles are particularly important:

1. A contract must have a *reasonable way of opting out*: In particular, it must be possible to choose to reject the contract, without giving up something that one has a right to. This is a consequence of the condition that *agreement* must be voluntary. In the case of the "social contract," however, there is no reasonable way of opting out. The only way of escaping subjection to government is to relocate to Antarctica.

2. *Explicit dissent trumps implicit consent*: The notion of implicit agreement (or disagreement) applies only in the absence of explicit statements. Thus, if a person *explicitly states* that they reject a certain arrangement, one cannot claim that the person implicitly accepted it. Yet in the case of the putative social contract, the state refuses to accept explicit dissent. However clearly you state your dissent, there is no way that the government will exempt you from its laws.

3. *Contractual obligations are mutual and conditional*: If two parties make a contract with each other, *both* parties must take on obligations to each other, and if either party repudiates their side of the deal, then the other party is no longer obligated to hold up their end. In the case of the alleged social contract, it is traditionally said that the government undertakes an obligation to protect individuals from criminals and foreign governments. In the United States, however, the government has explicitly rejected this. There are a number of court cases

in which citizens have sued government agencies, such as the police or the department of social services, for intentionally or negligently failing to protect individuals. In virtually every case, the government courts summarily dismiss the lawsuits, claiming that the government has no obligation to protect individuals. Here is a representative quotation from one of those court decisions, *Warren vs. District of Columbia*:

> Official police personnel and the government employing them are not generally liable to victims of criminal acts for failure to provide adequate police protection. . . . This uniformly accepted rule rests upon the fundamental principle that a government and its agents are under no general duty to provide public services, such as police protection, to any particular individual citizen.[5]

The judges' theory was that the government's duty is only to protect society in general, not any specific individual. Under standard contract doctrine, then, no specific individual would have any obligation to the government.

3   The Hypothetical Social Contract

3.1   Who Cares About Hypothetical Consent?

Some philosophers, after noticing that the social contract is a fiction, are not ready to give up on it yet. They instead move to the **hypothetical social contract theory**. This theory claims that, although we have not *actually* made an agreement to obey the state, we *would have* made such an agreement, assuming we were reasonable, were well informed, and were in an appropriate position for deciding on how our society should be organized. The fact that we would have made such an agreement is supposed to give both individuals and the state a reason for behaving as though the agreement was actually made.

---

5. 444 A.2d. 1, D.C. Ct. of Ap. 1981, at 4. The quotation is from the Superior Court decision, which the Appeals Court quoted approvingly.

Aside: John Rawls' Theory of Justice

John Rawls, the most influential political philosopher of the twentieth century, developed a theory of justice based upon a hypothetical social contract. Rawls asks us to imagine that the future members of a society meet to discuss the principles by which their society should be arranged. (This hypothetical situation is known as "the Original Position.") Suppose, however, that at the time they are discussing this, none of them knows what their own position in that society will be – nor, in fact, do they know any other personal details about themselves and their future lives. (Rawls calls this condition the "Veil of Ignorance.") This ensures that everyone would have to choose principles that would be fair to all. Assuming also that these people are reasonable, well informed (about matters *other than* the personal details about themselves), and rational, what would they agree to?

Rawls argues that they would agree to establish a system of the most extensive personal liberties possible compatible with everyone having the same liberties, and that they would agree to have the government redistribute wealth to the greatest benefit of the poorest class. Rawls then concludes that actual governments should follow those principles.

Rawls is the reason for the revival of interest in hypothetical contract theories in philosophy starting in the late twentieth century. Though Rawls does not explicitly deploy his approach to argue in favor of government in general (he instead simply assumes that there should be a government), the theory can obviously be applied to that question.

At first glance, it is not obvious how this is supposed to work. Usually, mere hypothetical agreements have no moral force. Suppose, for example, that one morning, you open your front door to find a copy of my book, *The Problem of Political Authority*, on your doorstep. Thinking that you've just been gifted a free copy, you go ahead and read it. The book turns out to be so clear, compelling, and intellectually amazing that it would easily have been worth the cover price of $40 if someone had been selling it. You count yourself lucky to have gotten it for free.

Two weeks later, I show up at your house, let you know that I was the one who left the book there, and insist that you *owe* me $40 for the book. Is this correct?

No, it isn't. Granted, it would be *nice* of you to pay me for my good work, but that isn't the question. The question is whether you are *obligated* to do so. You are not obligated to give me anything, because you never in fact promised to pay anything, neither implicitly nor explicitly. If I wanted payment, it was up to me to inform you of the price *in advance* and make sure that you agreed. My failure to do so means that I simply *gave* you the book.

It seems as though the same should be true of the government and its services. You might, indeed, have agreed to pay for the government's services *if* they had asked you in advance. But as they never asked you, it would seem that you are under no actual *obligation* to pay them anything. Of course, it would be *prudent* to pay them, since otherwise, they may send armed men to your house to kidnap and imprison you. But that is just a point about self-interest; that is quite a different matter from your having a *moral obligation* to pay them.

3.2 Hypothetical Consent in Common-Sense Morality

In spite of what I have just said, there are *some* cases in which hypothetical consent is morally efficacious, that is, it has an effect similar to actual consent. Consider that, in general, when a doctor performs surgery on a patient, the doctor needs the patient's *consent* to the surgery in advance. Now, suppose that you are the surgeon on duty in the emergency room of the local hospital. Suppose an accident victim has just been brought in who needs immediate surgery to save his life. This patient, however, is unconscious; hence, it is impossible to get his consent to the surgery. What should you do?

Everyone knows the answer. You do the surgery. Why? Because you know the patient almost certainly *would* agree to have it if the patient were able to do so. This shows that appeals to hypothetical consent *sometimes* succeed.

It is, however, crucial to the case that the patient is *unable* to consent due to unconsciousness. If the patient is *able* to understand the situation and respond to your questions, then you have to get his consent – you can't simply move directly to anesthetizing and then operating on him, on the ground that "he probably would consent if I asked him."

Now in the case of the hypothetical social contract, the citizens are not in fact unconscious. We are (almost all of us) perfectly aware and perfectly able to respond. The government could easily ask citizens for their consent. The reason they do not do so is obvious: they are afraid that too many people would refuse consent, and the government does not want to exempt those people from paying taxes or obeying other laws. Since the state intends to impose the same demands on you whether you consent or not, they see no point in asking if you consent. This would be like a surgeon who just straight away chloroforms patients when they come in the door and performs whatever medical procedures she deems necessary because she is afraid that the patients might not consent if she actually asked them.

Now, would we really consent to the social contract if we were given the choice? The answer, of course, is that some people would consent, and others would not. *How many* people would consent? It's hard to say. If the result of not consenting was that you didn't have to pay any taxes, I suspect that quite a lot of people would refuse consent. (The government, of course, could announce that it would not offer its protection to those people. So they would have to fend for themselves, hire private security guards, etc. This would still be worth it to many people.) Besides the large number of people who simply don't want to pay the monetary price of government, there would also be a smaller number of people who would refuse consent for ideological reasons, that is, because they are philosophically opposed to the government.

So the hypothetical social contract theory has two major problems. First, there is no reason to think that everyone would consent to the social contract. Second, this hypothetical consent would not matter even if it were true that everyone would consent: if it is feasible to ask for someone's actual consent to some arrangement, then one must do so, rather than merely hypothesizing that they would consent if asked.

3.3   Fairness and Reasonableness

There is another account of the relevance of hypothetical consent that we should address. The philosopher John Rawls argues that hypothetical consent is morally relevant, not because it is a second-best substitute when actual consent is unavailable (as in the example of the unconscious accident victim), but because hypothetical consent shows us something about what is *reasonable* or *fair*. That is, provided that we design our hypothetical scenario in the right way, we can be assured that whatever people in our hypothetical scenario would agree to is reasonable and fair to everyone. This fairness and reasonableness is the underlying reason why the terms of the hypothetical agreement should be followed in reality.[6]

The problem is that fairness and reasonableness cannot do the kind of moral work needed in this case. What kind of "moral work" is needed? Recall that the Problem of Political Authority arises in the first place because the government is engaged in activities that would be considered wrongful, indeed, as violations of individual rights, if anyone else were to do them. For instance, if you acted like the government, you'd be called a thief, a kidnaper, and a terrorist. So, to give a defense of political authority, one needs to cite some fact about the government that would somehow suspend or outweigh individual rights. Appeals to "fairness" and "reasonableness" do not do that.

To see my point, consider another hypothetical, which I will call "The Case of the Reasonable Job Offer": you are about to graduate from college. I offer you a job, doing exactly the kind of work that you told me you hope to be able to do (whatever that is – you fill in the details). The pay is excellent, there are opportunities for advancement, you'd be working with charming and fascinating people, and you presently have no other job prospects that are anywhere near as attractive. My job offer, in brief, is completely *fair* and more than *reasonable*. Indeed, let us suppose, it would be utterly unreasonable for you to reject it.

But suppose that you're just feeling unreasonable that day. And so you decide, in a fit of sheer pique, to *reject* my offer. Question: Is it now permissible for me to *force* you to take the job?

The answer to that is uncontroversial: No. I can't force you to work for me; that's called "slavery." But remember: the original job offer was eminently *fair* and *reasonable*. What this example shows is that fairness and reasonableness do not suffice to override individual rights. Individuals have the right to decide whom to work for or not work for. It doesn't matter if the contract was fair and reasonable; if the other party does not *in fact* accept it, then

6. Rawls 1999, pp. 15–19; Nagel 1991, pp. 33–40.

I can't impose it on them. And the same should apply to the social contract: it doesn't matter if the hypothetical *social* contract is fair and reasonable; if individuals have not *in fact* accepted it, then the state has no right to impose it on them.

Now, you might worry that I am drawing on the extreme negative associations of slavery for this example, and overgeneralizing to the conclusion that *no* rights-violating behavior can be justified by appeals to fairness and reasonableness. But it is not an overgeneralization; similar intuitions can be drawn from other cases involving all sorts of other seeming rights-violations. We could take a case of a trivial rights-violation and make a parallel point. For instance, suppose I make a completely fair and reasonable offer to sell you a high-quality sandwich for the low price of $2.50. In a fit of pique, you unreasonably reject the offer. I may not then *force* you to buy the sandwich. I can't steal the $2.50 from you and then leave you with the sandwich – even though it is a trivial rights-violation, and even though the trade would have been fair and reasonable if you had accepted it.

3.4 Dissenters

I said near the beginning (Section 1.4) that this chapter wasn't going to be about anarchism, and it isn't. But I am still going to mention anarchism here. But the only point that I need to make about it is this: there are at least some people who believe in it. Not very many, but there are some people who sincerely, and after serious reflection, believe that the best arrangement for society would be one without a government. For the point I want to make now, you don't have to *agree* with those people; you just have to agree that *they exist*.

That is enough to raise the other big, obvious problem for the hypothetical social contract theory: in fact, not everyone *would* accept the social contract. The anarchists would obviously reject it. This is a problem for social contract theories because a contract generally requires the agreement of *all parties* who are supposed to be bound by it. If you have a contract that is supposed to be binding on Alice, Bob, and Charles, then Alice, Bob, and Charles have to sign it. If only Alice and Bob sign it, then Alice and Bob may be bound by its terms, but Charles is not. So, on the face of it, it seems that anarchists are not bound by the social contract; hence, they would have no special obligations to obey the law or pay taxes, nor would the state have any special entitlement to force them to obey.

This is certainly not the result that defenders of authority want. They want the government's authority to extend to *everyone* within "the government's" territory. By the way, if being an anarchist resulted in not having to pay taxes, then a lot more people would probably become anarchists.

One way of handling this problem, for hypothetical contract theorists, would be to declare that only the agreement of *reasonable* people is required.[7] This would make sense if the theory's central argument is an appeal to fairness and reasonableness, as suggested in Section 3.3. The contract theorist might then argue that anarchists are "unreasonable," and therefore, their dissent does not matter.

There are, however, no objective, non-question-begging criteria by which anarchists are unreasonable. Of course, if you assume that government is justified, and you also stipulate that anyone who disagrees with something that is justified is "unreasonable," then you can conclude that anarchists are unreasonable – but that is begging the question. If one tries to use impartial criteria, anarchists are about as reasonable as any other political partisans and more reasonable than many. (To verify this, go read some anarchist writings.)[8] They give logical arguments, taking account of both empirical evidence and common-sense moral intuitions. They rationally respond to objections. They appeal to the common good, justice, and other impartial values. Of course, some people raise objections to their views, but that is true of *all* political views. The objections to anarchism are not particularly more powerful on their face than the objections to other political ideologies (indeed, I would say they are generally much less so). Most of the people who consider anarchism unreasonable are people who have dismissed anarchism without ever reading anything by any anarchist writer; in other words, they refuse to listen to the anarchists' reasons. So who are really the unreasonable ones?

Of course, there is no difficulty in showing that all reasonable people agree with you, as long as you define "reasonable" to include only people who agree with you. But this is scarcely an interesting conclusion.

---

7. See Scanlon 1998, pp. 5, 208–209; Nagel 1991, p. 36; Rawls 2005, p. 137.
8. For a helpful collection of writings on anarchism, see Stringham 2007.

3.5 Conclusion

In summary, the hypothetical social contract theory requires two premises to justify state authority:

1. Everyone (or all reasonable people) in a certain hypothetical scenario *would* agree to have a government, to obey its laws, and to pay taxes.
2. If everyone (or all reasonable people) would agree to this, then everyone is obligated to go along with it, and it is permissible to forcibly impose it on them, including people who have not *actually* agreed to it.

From these, it follows that we are all obligated to obey the state, and it is permissible for the state to forcibly impose laws on us. There are two problems with this argument: first, there is no reason to believe premise (1); second, there is no reason to believe premise (2). Indeed, as we have seen, both are obviously false.

4 Democratic Authority

4.1 Democracy as Majority Rule

The need for unanimous agreement is the bane of social contract theories. A more practical theory would be one that requires only the agreement of a *majority* of people – that, at least, is sometimes attainable. Indeed, this is one of the first things that people (in democratic countries) come up with when asked to explain what differentiates the state from a gang of criminals: the leaders of the government were chosen by a majority of the people.

How is this supposed to work to defend the authority of the state? It looks as though the implicit reasoning is something like the following:

1. In a democratic society, the laws are supported by the majority of people.
2. If something is supported by the majority of people, then it is obligatory to go along with it, and it is permissible to forcibly impose it on everyone, including those who do not agree with it.
3. Therefore, in a democratic society, it is obligatory to obey the laws, and it is permissible to forcibly impose those laws on everyone.

This argument is, on its face, completely unconvincing. Premise 2 is obviously false. Premise 1 is also dubious, though less obviously so. Let's start with premise 1. There are many reasons why the laws, even in a democratic country, may not, in fact, reflect the will of the majority. Occasionally, there is a prominent, unpopular bill that nevertheless passes the legislature, such as the infamous $700 billion bank bailout that the U.S. government passed in 2008. That, however, is an unusual case. The usual case is that the legislature passes laws that almost no one else in the country has even heard of, let alone has detailed knowledge of. The majority of Americans do not even know their congressman's name, and – except in a few special cases – virtually no one can say how their representative voted on the last issue to come before the legislature. This pervasive ignorance means that political leaders have a wide leeway in how they can behave; they do not have to strictly adhere to the will of the majority of voters.

Most defenders of democracy will want to argue that it is not necessary that every law be supported by the majority of people. It is enough that each law is supported by the majority of *legislators*, *and* that each of these legislators is overall supported by the majority of the people they are supposed to represent, as demonstrated in the elections. But even this weaker condition may not be met in reality for a variety of reasons, including the following:

1. Voters commonly find themselves with a limited range of choices at the ballot box, none of whom truly matches their preferences. They may vote for a candidate not because they actually approve of or agree with that candidate, but merely because they deem that candidate the lesser of two evils (or the least of three evils, etc.).
2. Voters are not given any choice about the general structure of government. One is simply born into a particular system, and one is then asked only to help choose the personnel who will occupy certain positions.
3. Political leaders often engage in tactics designed to skew election results. The most famous of these in the United States is the practice of "gerrymandering," in which the party in power redraws district boundaries – often in bizarre shapes – in order to maximize the number of districts wherein their party has a majority of voters and thus to maximize the

party's representation in the legislature. Another well-known tactic in U.S. elections is to attempt to foster cynicism among voters in the opposing party so that fewer of them turn out to vote.

4. In the United States and other modern democracies, most laws are not made by elected officials. Most laws are made by *bureaucrats*. The legislature creates a regulatory agency, gives it some broad mandate, and directs the bureaucrats to fill in the details. Another large body of law (case law) is made by judges, most of whom are also unelected. So the laws themselves are not directly chosen by the voters, nor are they made by people who were chosen by the voters, but they are made by people who were chosen by people who were chosen by the voters.

5. In some cases, representation is nonproportional. Thus, in the U.S. Senate, each state has equal representation despite extremely unequal population sizes. Wyoming, with under 600,000 people, has the same number of senators as California, with its nearly 40 million people (68 times more people than Wyoming).

6. In most democracies, large numbers of citizens fail to vote. In the typical American election, roughly half of people eligible to vote actually do so.

7. Most presently existing laws are leftover from earlier times. Thus, present-day citizens are bound by the decisions of *past* legislators, who may or may not be supported by the present population.

I have a specific point to make with these observations. I am not just vaguely complaining about all of these things. My point is that the laws in real-world democracies *do not necessarily reflect the will of the majority* of people. Defenders of political authority would want to claim that the law retains its authority in general. But it is difficult to see how they are going to get to this conclusion if the starting point is something about the importance of respecting the will of the majority.

In other words, even if you think there is something of deep moral import in the idea of democracy, real-world democracies are not all *that* democratic. Each of the aforementioned seven points calls into question the extent to which our laws are truly democratically authorized.

4.2 The Irrelevance of Majority Will

Now I propose to leave the topic of what the majority has or has not authorized because there is a clearer, more decisive point to make. Even if the laws are democratically authorized (whatever that might amount to), that fact is simply morally irrelevant – it does nothing to give the government any special authority. This is because the will of a majority does not suffice to cancel or outweigh the rights of a minority. An action that is normally impermissible does not suddenly become alright merely because most people support it.

Consider a hypothetical example, which I call the Democratic Dinner Party: I go out for dinner with four students. At the end of the meal, there is a debate about how the bill should be divided up, a topic we have not previously discussed. I propose that each person should pay for the items that he or she ordered. Three of the students, however, make the alternative proposal that *I* should be forced to pay for the entire meal. Since they are a majority, am I now *morally obligated* to pay for their meals? And are they entitled to *force* me to do so? If I refuse, may they kidnap me and lock me in a cage?

No, I am not obligated to pay for everyone, and they are not entitled to force me to do so. This example shows that majority will does not cancel or outweigh individual rights. In this case, my right to my own money and my general liberty right are not canceled or outweighed merely because a majority of the group wants to take away my money or imprison me.

This example is on point because, again, what we need from a theory of political authority is an explanation for why the state should be entitled to engage in behavior that would be deemed to violate individual rights if performed by anyone other than the government. Thus, it is fair to consider an example of an action that initially appears to violate someone's rights and then ask whether the moral situation is changed by the fact that a majority of people support the action. If (as we have just seen) the answer is no, then the purported fact that the government is supported by a majority of people cannot suffice to justify the government's seemingly rights-violating behavior.

There are, of course, much worse rights-violations that have been democratically authorized in history. For instance, in its early years, America democratically enacted laws enforcing slavery. Germany in 1932 democratically elected Nazis to a plurality of seats in the

Reichstag. These sorts of cases make the point that the democratic process does not have *unlimited* authority since presumably these particularly awful outcomes are not legitimate. But these sorts of examples do not suffice to rebut the belief in democratic authority in general, because most defenders of democratic authority are not *absolutists* about it. In Section 1.3, I allowed that defenders of authority need not endorse *all* laws made by the state (even a generally legitimate state). They may hold that some particularly awful laws are wrong to enforce and apt for disobedience by citizens. Most defenders of authority would respond to the examples of slavery and Nazi Germany by saying that those are cases where the laws, or other official government actions, are so awful that they lose their authority.

That is why my example of the Democratic Dinner Party is useful. Defenders of authority could not respond in the same way to that example – they could not say that forcing me to pay for everyone's dinner is such a horrific rights violation that it cancels or outweighs the authority that the democratic process normally carries. They could not say this because precisely the same sort of rights violation is involved in the maintenance of *all* actual governments. All governments force people to pay for services for the group; they call this policy "taxation," and it would be difficult to maintain a government without it. Yet the Democratic Dinner Party example shows that majority will does not suffice to override property rights.

4.3   The Importance of Deliberation

Some political philosophers appeal to the importance of democratic *deliberation*, arguing that an ideal deliberative process would confer authority on its results. If we all deliberate in a suitably rational, well informed, egalitarian, etc., manner, and we let this deliberation guide our voting choices, then the outcome of this process will be legitimate and all should go along with the collective decisions thereby made.[9]

There are two problems with this approach as a way of deriving political authority. The first problem is that no society employs anything remotely like an ideal deliberative process. It is well known

---

9. Cohen 1989; Habermas 2002.

that most voters in actual democracies are extremely ignorant, often irrational, and driven more by vague emotional associations and tribal affiliations than by rational deliberation.[10] Again, most Americans do not know their congressional representative's *name*, so it seems unlikely that they are in a position to ideally deliberate about that person's qualifications.

The second problem with the deliberative democracy approach is that deliberation, however well conducted, does not erase or render moot the rights of the individual. To see the point, imagine the following modification to the story of the Democratic Dinner Party from Section 4.2: suppose that the students conduct a lengthy *discussion* of whether I should be forced to pay for everyone's meal. This discussion satisfies all the norms for a well-conducted discussion that you might hope for. Everyone (including me) has a fair chance to explain their point of view, everyone listens respectfully to everyone else's arguments, and so on (include whatever conditions you think would make for a good deliberative process). *Then* they vote and the majority turn out to be in favor of forcing me to pay for everyone. So *now* am I morally obligated to pay for everyone, and are they morally entitled to force me to pay, because they deliberated very well before deciding to do it?

Surely not. This example shows that, just as mere majority will does not override individual rights, neither does well-conducted deliberation.

4.4 The Value of Equality

Some political philosophers argue that *equality* is a value of crucial import – in particular, that there is an imperative to treat all members of society as equals – and that democratic government is the only way to realize this value.[11] Democracy treats everyone as equals because everyone gets one vote. By contrast, if you refuse to go along with a democratically authorized law, then you are refusing to treat the other members of society as equals. You are in effect treating your own judgment or desires as being of greater weight than the judgment or desires of other people, since *most* people support the law.

---

10. Caplan 2007; Brennan 2016; Achen and Bartels 2016.
11. Christiano 2008.

I see three problems with this argument. First, the argument assumes that democratically made laws are, indeed, supported by the majority. As I argued in Section 4.1, this often is not the case. If the foundation of political authority lies in majority will, then we should be entitled to disobey unpopular laws, and government agents should not be entitled to enforce them.

Second, the argument seems to conflate different notions of equality. It is plausible that we are obligated to treat all people as equals in the sense of recognizing *the same rights* for all people. But it is completely implausible that we are obligated to "treat all people as equals" if that means treating everyone's *beliefs* as equally likely to be *true*, or treating everyone's expressed *preferences* as equally *reliable* indicators of what is morally right or good. That is completely implausible for a number of reasons, including the fact that some people are much more intelligent than others, some are much better informed than others about any given issue, some have spent much more time reflecting on a given issue than others, some have exerted much more effort to identify the morally correct result than others, and so on. Many political positions that voters adopt are taken up in an extremely casual way, with little to no reflection, and little to no concern about the rights of others. (Indeed, many voters do not even know what positions their favored candidate has adopted.) It cannot be obligatory to treat such positions as being reliable indicators of moral truth since they *obviously aren't*.

Third, the obligation to treat others as equals in this sense cannot cancel or outweigh the rights of the individual. Again consider the Democratic Dinner Party. Imagine that, after I decline to pay for everyone's meal, one of the students tries to persuade me by arguing as follows:

> Professor Huemer, surely you recognize that all people are created equal. Therefore, you are obligated to treat *us*, your fellow diners, as equals. That means that you have to give our normative judgments and preferences equal weight to your own. In this case, that means that you have to pay for everyone's meal; otherwise, you are treating your own preferences as more important than other people's preferences.

Notice that this speech would be parallel to the appeal on behalf of the democratic government. Yet surely it falls flat. However nice it might be to respect my students' judgments, that does not overrule my rights over my own money. It is part of the notion of property rights that one may do as one chooses with one's own property, without having to submit to the judgments or desires of others. That includes deciding to spend one's money on oneself, rather than on one's students. If we say that this amounts to treating others as "unequal" to oneself, then we can only conclude that it is permissible to treat others as unequal in that manner.

4.5   Conclusion

The laws in real-world democracies do not necessarily reflect the will of the majority of people. This fact poses a problem for arguments that try to justify political authority by appealing to the ideal of majority rule.

More importantly, the example of the Democratic Dinner Party shows that majority rule cannot justify political authority. If an action is of a kind that would normally violate the rights of an individual, that action is not rendered justified merely by the preferences of a larger group, nor is it justified if the group first deliberates in a special way before deciding to do it, nor is it justified by the need to treat persons as equals.

5   Utility and Fairness

5.1   A Utilitarian Case for Authority

Many people believe that government is incredibly beneficial and that without it, we would be doomed to a constant state of violent conflict, a war of all against all.[12] Can this belief be parlayed into a defense of political authority? We might argue as follows:

1.   General social order is extremely important.
2.   The maintenance of social order requires (a) that the state make and coercively enforce rules on the rest of society and (b) that individuals obey those rules.
3.   Therefore, the state should make and coercively enforce rules, and individuals should obey them.

---

12. For the classic statement of this view, which many people still accept, see Hobbes [1651] 1991.

The idea behind the first premise is that a general breakdown of social order would be so catastrophic that the government is justified in doing what is necessary to prevent that outcome, even if that means violating some individual rights here and there. In addition, individuals are obligated to do what is necessary to prevent the breakdown of social order. Premise 2 tells us that to prevent the breakdown of social order, the state must coercively enforce laws and individuals must obey those laws. Hence, the state and individuals should do those things.[13]

To illustrate the reasoning, consider the Lifeboat Case: you and a group of other people are stuck on a lifeboat in the middle of the ocean. The boat is taking on water and is in danger of sinking unless a sufficient number of people get to work bailing it out. For whatever reason, however, not enough other passengers are willing to bail out the boat voluntarily. Perhaps some of them don't believe it needs to be done at all, while others are simply hoping to sit back and let someone else do the work. In this situation, it seems that you would be justified in threatening the other passengers with physical violence in order to compel them to bail out the boat, since this is, regrettably, the only way to save everyone from drowning. In addition, it seems that individual passengers have some obligation to help bail out the boat.

The defender of authority thinks that the government is in an analogous position to you in this example. The threat of a sinking lifeboat is analogous to the threat of a breakdown of social order; forcing people to bail water is analogous to forcing people to obey the law.

5.2 The Problem of Legitimacy

Does this establish political authority? Not yet. Recall that the doctrine of political authority has two components: political legitimacy and political obligation. Let's start with the notion of political legitimacy.

To defend political legitimacy, we need an argument for a content-independent, special prerogative on the part of the state

---

13. This is roughly David Hume's [1777] 1987 view of authority, which he advances after refuting the social contract theory.

to forcibly impose rules on individuals. Now, the reasoning of Section 5.1 might justify the state in coercively imposing some laws on the rest of society. But it would not justify imposing just *any* laws. On its face, the argument only justifies imposing those laws that are *necessary for maintaining social order*. This is not content-independent – whether a given law contributes to maintaining social order depends on the content of the law. Laws prohibiting theft and personal violence would clearly be justified by the argument of Section 5.1. The overwhelming majority of actual laws, however, are not necessary or even helpful for maintaining social order.

In the present-day United States, for example, there are laws designed to stop recreational drug use, restrict who can practice medicine, control the price of labor, redistribute wealth from the rich to the poor, control how foods are labeled, subsidize corn farmers, maintain national parks, support the arts, explore outer space, limit immigration, control what children are taught in schools, discourage tobacco smoking, provide pensions for retirees, and so on. These laws are more or less irrelevant to maintaining social order – society could be equally orderly without them.

Some government programs are *claimed* (by the government) to be helpful for maintaining security but may actually be counterproductive – such as the U.S. government's torture program in the 2000s or the 2003 invasion of Iraq. Without entering into a debate concerning those specific policies, I would point out that the argument of Section 5.1 does not lend any support to an entitlement to impose counterproductive or otherwise harmful policies.

So there are two related constraints on the state's entitlement to coercively impose rules. The first is a subject-matter constraint: the rules must be relevant to maintaining social order and preventing the sort of catastrophe that would allegedly result from anarchy. The other is a correctness constraint: the rules must actually be beneficial or reasonably expected to be beneficial. Since these constraints are content-*dependent*, we have not found a defense of *authority* as defined in Section 1.2.

To illustrate, imagine the following modifications to the Lifeboat Case from Section 5.1. You have just successfully forced the other passengers to bail out the lifeboat, as discussed. Now that that's taken care of, imagine that you move on to seizing a wealthy passenger's wallet to give her money to a poorer passenger; demanding that another passenger stop eating potato chips because they are bad for his health; forcing everyone on the lifeboat to pray to Poseidon, the god of the ocean; and throwing overboard another passenger who looks shifty to you. Are these further actions of yours morally legitimate?

Obviously not. This illustrates that the necessity of using force to prevent some catastrophe does not create any general *authority* in the sense defined in Section 1. The fact that you had to use force to save the lifeboat from sinking does not mean that you now have a general entitlement to force others to obey your will. You are entitled only to use the minimum force needed to prevent the lifeboat from sinking. Once you have gotten the passengers to bail out the boat, you have to stop the coercion. You can't stop them from eating potato chips, because this is not relevant to keeping the boat afloat (nor to any other sufficiently urgent impending disaster). You also cannot make everyone pray to Poseidon because there is not sufficient evidence for thinking that this is beneficial. Likewise, the government has no general right to deploy coercion for purposes unrelated to maintaining social order, nor for the sake of policies for which we lack sufficient evidence of their usefulness. When they do these things, we should view them in the same way that we view criminal gangs.

5.3   The Problem of Political Obligation

The Irrelevance of Individual Action

Let us turn now to the alleged obligation on the part of citizens to obey the law. One might argue that disobedience to the law – even unjustified laws – threatens social order, and for this reason, individuals have a general obligation to obey the law.

But how much does an individual's disobedience really threaten the social order? There are literally *millions* of law-violations every year in the United States, and this has been true for many years. Indeed, we see much higher crime rates as we look further into the past. It therefore seems farfetched, to say the least, to suppose that an individual has the power to collapse social order through disobeying some laws. You could break ten laws every day for the rest of your life, and general social order would take no notice. It is, therefore, not obvious how appeals to the importance of maintaining social order can demonstrate an individual obligation to obey the law.

Of course, there are some laws that you should not break because they are supported by independent moral reasons. For instance, don't break the murder laws, because murder is, independently of the legal situation, morally wrong. But it is unclear why you should obey laws that are *not* supported by independent moral reasons. And *that* is what political authority is about. The core of the idea of authority is the legitimacy of the "because I said so" explanation for an imperative.

What If Everyone Did That?

In response to the preceding rather obvious point, proponents of authority often grant that a single individual cannot collapse social order, but they go on to ask, rhetorically, "What if everyone did that?" If *everyone* were to break the law *very often*, then social order might, indeed, collapse, depending on which laws were broken. Of course, disobeying the law does not cause everyone else to do the same thing. Nevertheless, some believe that it is morally wrong to behave in a certain way if you know that it would be terrible if everyone behaved that way. In line with this thought, some philosophers hold that the morally right thing to do is to follow the *general rules* that would have the best consequences if everyone were to follow them. You can't control what everyone else does, but you can do your part.

Here is an illustration to help make this principle plausible. Return to the Lifeboat case, in which the lifeboat needs to be bailed out to prevent it from sinking. This time, remove the idea of coercion and suppose that people are voluntarily bailing. Now suppose that the lifeboat can stay afloat as long as *most* people help to bail it out, which they are in fact doing; thus, if just *you* refuse to help, the boat will still remain afloat. In this case, is it alright for you to just sit back, playing games on your phone and watching the other passengers do all the work?

Most people intuit that this is not alright. You should help to bail the boat, even though your individual contribution doesn't make any noticeable difference to the boat's chances of staying afloat. Plausibly, the reason why it is wrong to just sit back and watch has something to do with the fact that it would be bad if everyone just sat back and watched.

In a similar manner, perhaps it is wrong to disobey the law, even though your individual action will make no noticeable difference to general social order, because it would be bad if everyone behaved in the same manner.

The Need for Fairness

So, the principle we're considering (you should not do things that would be bad for everyone to do) has some intuitive force. Nevertheless, the principle cannot be accepted without qualification. That's because there are many things that it is perfectly alright to do, or even *praiseworthy* to do, even though it would be terrible if everyone did them. For example, suppose you are considering pursuing a career as a firefighter. While you're thinking about this prospect, it occurs to you to ask yourself, "What if everyone did that?" You quickly realize that it would be terrible if *everyone* became a firefighter. There would be no farmers, so we'd have no food; no construction workers, so we'd have no houses; no doctors, so no medical care; no truck drivers, so no deliveries; no philosophers, so no amazing books like this one to befuddle people; and so on. Does this show that it's morally wrong to become a firefighter? Of course not. In fact, it is *praiseworthy* to become a firefighter. This shows that it cannot be wrong *in general* to behave in a way that you wouldn't want everyone else to behave.

So, when is it alright to do the things that you wouldn't want everyone to do, and when is it not alright? Here, I will just suggest a general, vague answer that seems right to me: I think it is wrong to do X, provided that (i) it would be bad if everyone did X *and* (ii) it would be *unfair* for *you* to do X while *other* people refrain. Of course, what counts as unfair is often open to debate. Nevertheless, we will not need a detailed account of unfairness because we will not have to rely on any particularly controversial applications of condition (ii); it will suffice to rely on common-sense intuitions.

Thus, to return to the earlier examples, it is, intuitively, *unfair* for you to sit back and watch while other people do all the work of bailing out the lifeboat. On the other hand, it is not at all unfair for you to become a firefighter while other people pursue other professions. This explains why refusing to help bail water is wrong, while becoming a firefighter is perfectly alright.

Is Disobedience Unfair?

So the question now is whether it is unfair for you to disobey the law while other members of your society obey.

In the case of the tax laws, the fairness claim is very plausible. Some amount of taxes have to be paid to maintain social order, which benefits everyone (for now, let's ignore all the other things the government does that aren't necessary for maintaining social order). If some people evade their taxes, that means that the rest of the people have to pay *more*. This, in general, seems unfair. (Caveat: it might not be unfair if the share of taxes that one was legally required to pay was unfairly high to begin with, and if one's tax evasion merely resulted in one's paying a more reasonable, fairer share of the tax burden. But let's set aside this point as well.)

The issue I want to focus on is whether disobedience to the law, apart from the tax laws, is in general unfair to other citizens. In the abstract, it might seem plausible that it is, particularly if we think of obedience to the law as a sacrifice of one's liberty which a sufficient number of people have to make in order to maintain social order. But once we start looking at concrete examples, this superficial plausibility tends to evaporate.

Thus, suppose I want to smoke some crack cocaine to get high. I do this in the privacy of my own house, in my free time, with no one else around. I don't hurt anyone else, and indeed, no one else even knows about my crack habit (I make the cocaine myself at home). All of this is stipulated to remove any *independent* moral reasons against indulging my crack habit. My behavior is nevertheless highly illegal, and I have no very strong reasons for doing it. So, if there is a general obligation to obey the law just because it is the law, that obligation should apply to precisely this sort of case.

Now, could we plausibly claim that, when I light up my crack pipe, this is *unfair* to other people? Unfair to whom? All the non-crack smokers? Most other people don't *want* to smoke crack in the first place, so it is hard to see what is unfair to them about the fact that I'm smoking it and they are not.

Perhaps it is unfair to the other people who *want* to smoke crack but refrain from doing so because of the drug laws? But, if this is so, it seems that it is the *state*, not me, who is to blame for the unfairness – *they* are the ones stopping the would-be crack users from smoking. To blame *me* would be akin to blaming people who haven't been mugged for the unfairness experienced by mugging victims. It may in some sense be unfair that some people get mugged while others do not, but the only sensible remedy for this unfairness would be for fewer people to get mugged. One can hardly blame nonvictims for avoiding getting mugged by, for example, intentionally avoiding dangerous areas.

Perhaps what is unfair is that other people, in obeying the law, have sacrificed their personal liberty in order to maintain social order, while I have refused to do my share of liberty sacrificing. (Aside: I find it dubious that people really obey laws for that reason, but let's pretend that that's the case.) To make this plausible, however, we would have to assume that people's smoking crack in private, with no one else around, has some effect on general social order. It is hard to see how it does. And so, it is hard to see how refraining from smoking crack can be construed as part of "doing your part to maintain social order."

Notice that in other cases where we see unfairness in someone's failing to do their share in a cooperative scheme, the failure to do one's part actually has an effect on others. In the Lifeboat case, if you sit back and wait for others to bail water, that means that other people will have to do *more* bailing than they would if you had done your part. Similarly, in the case of taxation, if you evade your taxes, that means that other people have to pay more (tax rates, in general, are higher than they would be if there were 100% compliance with the tax laws). That makes it clear how the other people have a complaint against the noncooperator. But that is *not* true in the case of me with my crack pipe. It is not as if because I'm violating the drug laws in my house, now *other* people elsewhere in the country will have to obey *more* laws than they would have if I had "done my part" by obeying the drug laws. My obedience or disobedience to the drug laws has no effect on how much law-following other people will have to do.

There are *some* cases where my lawbreaking might have an effect on social order. If I am a famous public figure, and if I flout laws in a very public and reckless way, then it is possible that this would encourage disobedience by other people. Even if I only disobeyed bad laws, I might be prompting some others to disobey some good laws. It's possible that other public figures would then have to make extra efforts to try to forestall my ill effects on society. However, even if all this is true, this would be a special case. It gives no grounds for a *general* obligation for individuals to obey the law merely because it is the law.

5.4 Conclusion

Even if we think that government is necessary for maintaining social order, and even if we agree that widespread disobedience would threaten the social order, this provides no basis for belief in political authority, properly understood. The need for social order could not explain the state's putative entitlement to coercively impose policies that are not necessary for maintaining social order (which includes almost all actual policies), nor for imposing harmful, unjust, or otherwise poorly chosen policies. Nothing can account for a *general* entitlement to impose one's will on others.

The argument for political obligation runs into the problem that any given individual's behavior has no actual effect on general social order; hence, appeals to the need for social order don't seem to explain why any given individual must obey the law. The best way for the authority advocate to address this problem is probably to appeal to the principle that it is wrong to do something if (i) it would be bad if everyone behaved in that way *and* (ii) it is unfair for you to behave in that way while other people do not. In some cases, it could plausibly be argued that this principle supports obeying the law. But in many other cases, there is nothing particularly unfair to anyone about failing to obey the law. Hence, there is no reason to believe in a general, content-independent duty to obey laws.

We of course cannot review all possible arguments for political authority. At this point, however, we have reviewed the four most popular arguments endorsed by believers in authority. They were the (actual) social contract theory, the hypothetical social contract theory, the democratic theory, and the utilitarian/fairness theory. None of these theories succeeds in explaining the state's authority. These theories fail due to a mixture of obviously false factual assumptions (e.g., "we all made a contract to obey the state") and obviously false moral assumptions (e.g., "if most people want something, that makes it okay").

The best explanation for the abject failure of these accounts of authority is that they are rationalizations for a prejudice – the prejudice in favor of the status quo and in favor of the interests of the powerful. On reflection, the idea that some people have a special property called "authority" that means that everyone else has to obey their will, even when they give foolish or immoral commands, is quite strange. If we can't seem to explain why anyone has that property, that is probably because no one does. There are just some people who have acquired *power* over others – the ability to bring to bear sufficient force to bend others to their will. These people then invent rationalizations for their coercive behavior, which they use to try to convince everyone else to accept their dominance cheerfully.

6   So What If There Is No Authority?

In this section, I'm going to discuss the implications of rejecting political authority. If there is no authority, how should the government change its policies? How should government officials such as police and judges behave? How should juries behave? And how should ordinary individuals behave?

6.1   Policy Implications

Though the state may lack authority, it is not going away any time soon. Given that we have a state, but that the state lacks political authority, what sorts of policies should it adopt?

The absence of genuine authority does not mean that the state may never use force. It means that the state is not *above* the rest of us; it is subject to the same moral constraints as other agents are. Thus, the state is justified in using force only in circumstances and for reasons that would justify the use of force by any ordinary agent. It is widely accepted that there are *some* such circumstances. Of particular interest, an individual may use force to defend himself or an innocent third party from wrongful use of force by another. More generally, one may use force to defend against violations of someone's rights. If you see someone trying to kill your neighbor, you may come to his aid, even to the point of killing the aggressor if necessary. If someone breaks into your house and starts stealing your property, you may likewise use force to repel them. Obviously, there are some constraints: you should not use *excessive* force, you should not deploy force that is vastly more harmful than the harm you are defending against, and you should not use force at all if completely peaceful and effective alternatives are available. But with those qualifications understood, use of force is justified to defend the rights of yourself or third parties.

Thus, even without having "authority," the state may also use force to defend people's rights. This is the main task of the criminal law, the police, and the courts. The state may coercively enforce rules against theft, murder, rape, and other rights violations. They may also deploy force to repel foreign invasions.

There are, however, a great many actual government activities that are not justified. For example, the government in all or most countries has made it illegal to consume certain recreational drugs, mainly because these drugs are bad for the user. What if I were to behave in the same way as the state? I tell my neighbors that I have made a list of unhealthy substances that I forbid them to consume. When I find someone using one of these substances, I kidnap them at gunpoint and lock them in a cage for a period of years. Surely, this behavior on my part would be wrong. Therefore, if the state is subject to the same moral constraints as other agents, then this behavior is also wrong on the part of the state.

For another example, suppose I am running a charity that helps the poor. Unfortunately, I feel that I am not getting enough voluntary contributions, so I take to *demanding* money from my neighbors. If anyone refuses to pay the amount that I deem appropriate, I, again, kidnap them and lock them in a cage. This also seems wrong. But that is analogous to government social welfare programs – they are a kind of charity run by the state, for which the state collects forced donations. So, if we are to apply common-sense morality to the state, then government social welfare programs are morally wrong.

For a third example, suppose that there are two people, A and B, who are competing for a job. I decide that I would rather that A get the job than B. So, on the day that B is supposed to have his job interview, I get my M16 and bar the road, forcibly stopping B from getting to his interview. As a result, the employer hires A, and B winds up unemployed. This behavior on my part seems unacceptable. But that is analogous to the government's restrictions on immigration, given the most common rationale cited for such restrictions. Immigration laws block immigrants from entering the domestic labor market so that employers will hire native-born citizens instead of foreigners.

There are many more immoral laws that could be cited. Indeed, probably the vast majority of laws are morally wrong because they involve the government in deploying force against individuals for reasons that would not justify the use of force on the part of any ordinary agent. On my account, the most that can be justified is what is sometimes called "the minimal state" or the "night watchman state" – a government that limits itself to protecting citizens from violations of their rights by criminals and foreign governments.

6.2 Enforcing Unjust Laws

How should government officials behave when there is an unjust law? Should they faithfully enforce the law, or should they conscientiously refuse? For example, should police officers arrest drug users? Should prosecutors prosecute them, and judges sentence them?

The answer is that government officials should do their best to avoid enforcing unjust laws. If they can prevent other officials from enforcing the unjust laws as well, they should do that. Why? Because it's wrong to knowingly support injustice. That is self-evident. Officials should not enforce unjust laws for the same reason that I should not go kidnap my next-door neighbor right now and lock him in the basement.

That is not, however, the conventional view. Police officers, judges, and prosecutors generally think that they are bound to enforce the law. Probably, most ordinary citizens agree with them and do not blame them for enforcing unjust laws. This is mostly due to a background belief in political authority, which convinces people that intentional infliction of unjust harm is transformed into a just act as long as it is done by a government official in the course of their job.

Often, when confronted with the argument that it is wrong to cause unjust harm, people will appeal to "the job" of a government official. For example, it is said that it is not the judge's *job* to evaluate whether the law is just; his job is only to enforce the law (and the same can be said of police and prosecutors). This argument supposes that faithfully executing one's job is important enough to outweigh the moral reasons against inflicting unjust harm on other people. But what exactly is meant by something's being or not being "one's job"?

We could interpret the phrase literally – one's job is what one gets paid for doing. For example, judges are not paid by the government for exercising their moral judgment about the laws; they are paid for enforcing the government's laws. But it is hard to see how this sort of appeal could be thought to justify an action that would otherwise be unjust. "I am being paid to do it!" is not, in general, a great moral defense of behavior that inflicts unjust harm on others.

Suppose you meet a Mafia hit man. You tell the hit man that he should stop murdering people. He responds, "I am just doing my job. My job is not to judge whether murder is right or wrong; my job is just to murder the people whom the boss wants dead." The hit man's claims are completely factually accurate – his job is, indeed, to murder people targeted by the boss, and his job most definitely does not include having a conscience. Yet this is, to say the least, a poor moral defense of his behavior. If a certain type of action is normally wrong, it does not become permissible just because someone pays you to do it. Similarly, then, the fact that government officials are hired to implement unjust laws does nothing to render that behavior permissible.

Let's try another interpretation. Maybe the appeal to one's job is really an appeal to the requirements of a *socially accepted role*, within a generally beneficial institution. Since the Mafia is not a desirable institution in general, one has no justification for adopting a particular role within that organization; also, the role of Mafia hit man is not generally socially accepted. But the government is socially accepted and perhaps generally beneficial. Perhaps these facts explain why the Mafia hit man cannot appeal to his job requirements, yet a government official can.

Here, then, is another example. I work for a university, which is generally beneficial (let's assume). Many students learn useful things, have their minds expanded, learn to question authority, and so on. A fair number of these students even remember some of what they have learned after they graduate. Suppose also that at my university, there is a particular role called "Aggressor." The job of the Aggressor is to pick one freshman student each year, known as "the Victim," and make that student miserable. For instance, a good Aggressor might sneak into the Victim's dorm room while the Victim is asleep and pour a glass of cold water over the Victim's face. On another day, the Aggressor might lock the Victim in a pillory, to be publicly humiliated, have rotten fruit thrown at him all day, and so on. This, let us suppose, is a tradition that goes back for decades, indeed, to the very founding of the university. The community approves of all this because the community is filled with sadistic assholes. But, to repeat, the university is nevertheless *overall* beneficial because the good work that we do (teaching students about political philosophy and such) outweighs the suffering of the one Victim each year.

Question: is it now *morally okay* to play the role of Aggressor and to abuse students in these ways? Suppose I was elected to be the Aggressor for the year, and I have kidnaped my Victim to lock him in a pillory. The Victim protests vehemently at being locked in the pillory. Could I reasonably respond, "I am just doing my job. My job is not to exercise moral judgment; my job is to torment you"?

I think not. The claim may again be perfectly factually accurate – tormenting the Victim is, indeed, my socially approved role. But this does nothing to justify it. Immoral behavior does not become moral simply by being attached to some socially approved role. Similarly, then, enforcing unjust laws (which is usually *much* more harmful than locking someone in a pillory for a day) cannot be rendered moral merely by being associated with a socially approved role.

A related argument sometimes heard is that the system overall will do a better job of achieving just and beneficial outcomes if each person in the system strives to faithfully execute their assigned role, rather than exercising their own conscience. The main problem with this argument is that there is no reason to believe this. Why would justice be more likely to be attained if we *don't* try to attain it? That is not the way things normally work.

I don't mean to imply that that is in principle *impossible*. Here is one theoretically possible way that directly aiming at justice (or other moral values) could be counterproductive. Suppose there were some experts on justice and morality – perhaps there could be a bureau of leading government philosophers – and their moral judgment was much more reliable than that of nonexperts, due to their intelligence, education, long hours of study, and serious commitment to justice and the good. Suppose also that these experts had a central role in shaping the existing laws so that all or nearly all of the laws were things that a consensus of these experts deemed to be just. And suppose, finally, that you are a government official hired to enforce the laws, but that you yourself lack expertise in evaluating justice. In these conditions, it would be plausible to argue that, even when the law seems to you unjust, you should defer to the law – that that practice would be the most reliable way of pursuing justice.

Of course, those are not our actual conditions. It is a matter for debate whether there are such things as moral experts in general. But if there are, they most certainly do not play any central role in shaping government policy. If there are moral experts, they are probably either moral and political philosophers or exceptionally virtuous people (such as, say, Mahatma Gandhi or Mother Theresa). Neither class of people plays any significant role at all in determining government policy. Government policy is determined more by the balance of power among competing interest groups, the whims of uninformed voters, and the ideologies of politicians. There is no reason to think any of those forces has a tight connection to moral truth.

In short, we do not live under a system that is strongly oriented toward justice or morality. So, there is no reason to think that one would generally do better at pursuing justice by deferring to the existing laws than by consulting one's own conscience.

6.3 Jury Nullification

All of that (Sections 6.1–6.2) was about how government officials – legislators, judges, police officers, prosecutors – should behave. If you're reading this book, though, you are probably not a government official. It is more likely that you are a philosophy student, a scholar, or some other sort of intellectual. So, perhaps the preceding discussion is not particularly practically relevant for you.

But there is one way in which you are quite likely to be called upon to help enforce the law. This is through serving on a jury if you live in a country that recognizes the right to trial by jury. You will probably be asked at some point in your life, along with several other ordinary citizens, to determine the guilt or innocence of a criminal defendant. (You also might be called for jury service in a civil case, but let's leave that aside.) If you are, the judge will almost certainly tell you that "your job" is solely to evaluate the *factual evidence* in the case, and not to morally evaluate the law, the defendant's behavior, or anything else.

If this happens, here is what you should do. During the jury selection process, you should agree with everything the judge says and promise to follow his instructions. Only then you will actually be seated on a jury. Then, once you begin deliberating in the jury room, you should disregard the judge's instructions and proceed to morally evaluate the case. In particular, you should reflect as carefully and rationally as possible on what is the *just* resolution of the case: does this defendant deserve to be punished? You should also look up what the punishment for the crime in question is so that you can morally assess whether that punishment is fair, since in many cases, particularly in the United States, the law requires shockingly draconian punishments.[14] If, after serious reflection, you judge that the punishment the defendant would most likely receive would be *just*, then you should vote "guilty." If not, then you should vote "not guilty."

---

14. For the sentencing guidelines applicable to most cases in the United States, see United States Sentencing Commission 2018.

If you actually do this, by the way, you should generally expect all the other jurors to disagree with you, since the overwhelming majority of citizens care less about justice than about obeying authority figures and the overwhelming majority of trials result in conviction. You will feel socially pressured to go along with conviction. Some jurors may become angry at you for taking up their time and for exercising your conscience instead of just obeying the authority figure. In explaining your position, you should also come up with some reasons for doubting the factual evidence, since the other jurors are more likely to listen to this. In effect, if the law or its prescribed punishment is unjust, then you should adopt an incredibly demanding standard of proof.

Aside: Unjust Trial Outcomes

Here are some examples of actual trial outcomes in the United States.

In the 1970s, Paul Lewis Hayes was prosecuted for attempting to pass a forged check for $88.[15] The prosecutor offered to recommend a sentence of five years in prison if Hayes would agree to plead guilty and "save the court the inconvenience and necessity of a trial." Hayes declined and insisted on his right to a trial. The prosecutor then secured a new indictment of Hayes under a habitual offender statute, which carried a mandatory minimum sentence of *life imprisonment* for a third conviction (Hayes had two prior felony convictions). Hayes was convicted at trial, sentenced to life imprisonment, and the sentence was upheld on appeal.

In 2007, Anthony Crutcher was arrested in Mississippi for selling $40 worth of cocaine to a police informant. In view of his two prior drug convictions, Crutcher was sentenced to 60 years in prison.[16]

---

15. *Bordenkircher v. Hayes*, 434 U.S. 357 (1978).
16. *Crutcher v. State of Mississippi et al.*, No. 2:2012cv00118 – Document 12 (N.D. Miss. 2012), retrieved April 14, 2020 from https://law.justia.com/cases/federal/district-courts/mississippi/msndce/2:2012cv00118/33395/12/.

In 2010, Larry Dayries committed "aggravated robbery" at a Whole Foods Market in Austin, Texas; specifically, Dayries was convicted of stealing a tuna fish sandwich and threatening a guard with a three-inch pocket knife in order to get away with the sandwich. No one was hurt. Due to his prior convictions for burglary and theft, Dayries was sentenced to 70 years in prison.[17]

These outcomes did not occur because the judges considered the sentences just. They occurred because the legislature passed statutes imposing blanket minimum sentences for certain offenders, especially repeat offenders. The legislators who voted for these laws never reviewed the specific cases mentioned and would almost certainly agree with everyone else that the sentences in those cases were unjust. Judges nevertheless hand down these sentences because they believe that they are obligated to enforce the law as written.

What I have just recommended is known as "jury nullification" – the practice wherein a jury effectively *nullifies* a law (renders it of no effect) by refusing to convict someone who obviously broke the law. Juries have done this occasionally for as long as there have been juries. For example, during the slavery era, juries often refused to convict defendants for violating the Fugitive Slave Laws (laws that required citizens to report escaped slaves). During the Prohibition era, they often refused to convict people for alcohol crimes. During the 1990s, Dr. Jack Kevorkian was acquitted three times of charges of assisted suicide (of which he was obviously guilty). Today, drug trials often result in hung juries due to widespread opposition to the nation's drug laws. Prosecutors and judges tend to be violently opposed to the practice of jury nullification although philosophers and legal scholars are much more likely to endorse it.

We can't discuss here all the arguments concerning jury nullification. I will just focus on the points connected to political authority. The absence of political authority means that there is no moral

---

17. *Larry Dayries v. The State of Texas* – Appeal from 147th District Court of Travis County, retrieved April 14, 2020 from https://law.justia.com/cases/texas/third-court-of-appeals/2011/20503.html.

magic that converts unjust harm into something moral and just when it is carried out by the state. When a person is convicted under an unjust law, that person will generally suffer severe, undeserved harm. When they are imprisoned, the harm that person suffers is just as bad as the harm suffered by an innocent person who is kidnaped and held hostage by a criminal gang. (Criminal gangs often abuse their hostages – but then, prisoners in the government's jails also often suffer abuse at the hands of guards and other prisoners.) A morally decent person should not knowingly inflict that kind of suffering on another person who does not deserve it. Indeed, a decent person should do his best to prevent unjust suffering, if he can do so relatively easily. That is the core reason for jury nullification. In short, it is wrong to knowingly cause unjust harm, and there is nothing that erases that wrongness when the unjust harm is delivered through the apparatus of the state.

What do opponents of jury nullification say? Some appeal to the jury member's "job." (Recall the "just doing my job" argument from Section 6.2.) They say that the jury's *job* is not to evaluate the law (that is the legislature's job); the jury's job is just to evaluate the factual evidence. There are two replies to this. First, as noted earlier, appeals to a person's "job" or socially defined role are not a way of circumventing morality. Immoral actions do not become moral as soon as someone creates a job for people who do them.

Second, in this case, the claim is factually false. The jury's job is *not* just to evaluate the factual evidence; the jury's job is to serve as the conscience of the community and as a check on government power. That is what the jury was originally intended to do, and this is made clear by many statements regarding the right to trial by jury made by the founders of the U.S. Constitution. Indeed, this is the only role that makes sense of the institution of trial by jury. If all we wanted was someone to faithfully apply the law to the factual evidence, then professional judges would be much better than random people off the street. The only reason why we might need the average people off the street – the only thing that might give these random people an advantage over professional judges – is if we want someone to serve as a *check on government power*. But that can only work if the jury stand prepared to nullify the law.[18]

---

18. For a more thorough discussion of jury nullification, see Huemer 2018.

Aside: Quotes About the Function of Juries

Judge Simon E. Sobeloff, *United States v. Moylan* (1969):

> If the jury feels that the law under which the defendant is accused is unjust, or that exigent circumstances justified the actions of the accused, or for any reason which appeals to their logic or passion, the jury has the power to acquit, and the courts must abide by that decision.[19]

Chief Justice John Jay, instructions to the jury in *Georgia v. Brailsford* (1794):

> It may not be amiss, here, Gentlemen, to remind you of the good old rule, that on questions of fact, it is the province of the jury, on questions of law, it is the province of the court to decide. But it must be observed that by the same law, which recognizes this reasonable distribution of jurisdiction, you have nevertheless a right to take upon yourselves to judge of both and to determine the law as well as the fact in controversy.[20]

John Adams on the responsibility of a juror:

> It is not only his right, but his duty to find the verdict according to his own best understanding, judgment, and conscience, though in direct opposition to the direction of the court.[21]

Thomas Jefferson, on his reservations about the French Revolution:

> Another apprehension is that a majority cannot be induced to adopt the trial by jury; and I consider that as the only anchor, ever yet imagined by man, by which a government can be held to the principles of its constitution.[22]

---

19. 417 F.2d 1002 (1969), at p. 1006.
20. 3 U.S. 1 (1794), p. 4.
21. Adams 1771, p. 8. Adams is discussing a case in which the judge gives instructions that, in the jury's opinion, conflict with the principles of the Constitution.
22. Jefferson 1789.

> Alexander Hamilton in the *Federalist Papers*, discussing the proposed Constitution:
>
> The friends and adversaries of the Constitution, if they agree in nothing else, concur at least in the value they set upon the trial by jury; or if there is any difference between them it consists in this: the former regard it as a valuable safeguard to liberty; the latter represent it as the very palladium of free government. . . . It would be altogether superfluous to examine . . . how much more merit it may be entitled to, as a defense against the oppressions of a hereditary monarch, than as a barrier to the tyranny of popular magistrates in a popular government.[23]

6.4   Civil Disobedience

Civil disobedience is a practice wherein individuals openly disobey the law or other government commands due to moral objections to the law, usually with the hope of prompting social change. Civil disobedience has been used successfully in many cases, most famously by Mahatma Gandhi in the movement for Indian independence from Britain and by Martin Luther King, Jr., in the U.S. civil rights movement.

Some thinkers worry a great deal about when civil disobedience is permissible and how it should be exercised to maintain proper respect for the law.[24] Some think that civil disobedience must be used only in extreme cases and that the disobedient subject must willingly accept punishment from the government, in order to demonstrate his respect for the law. Martin Luther King described civil disobedience together with the acceptance of punishment as "the very highest respect for the law."[25]

Those constraints, however, are groundless. There is no need for any special circumstances to justify civil disobedience. Since the

---

23. Hamilton 1788.
24. See Rawls 1999, pp. 319–343 (but note that I do not adopt Rawls' unduly restrictive definition of "civil disobedience").
25. Brooks 1965.

state has no authority, disobedience is justified by default. That is, it is permissible to disobey the law as long as there are no reasons for obeying. In addition, the idea of willingly accepting punishment from the state is, in most cases, irrational. If the law is unjust to begin with, then punishment under that law is also unjust – indeed, that punishment is normally the central locus of the injustice. Protesting injustice does not require willingly inviting injustice upon oneself. Breaking an unjust law and then *turning yourself in to be punished* is crazy. It is like a Jewish person seeking out a local skinhead gang and asking to be beaten up.

Of course, the locus of disagreement here is the idea of authority: I think it's crazy to turn yourself in because I think the state has no authority. Those who think civil disobedients should turn themselves in for punishment think so because they assume that the state has legitimate authority and thus has a right to punish those who violate its laws.

The rest of their position is hard to reconcile, however. If the state has legitimate authority, then how could the disobedience be justified to begin with? One might say that the state has legitimate authority *in general*, but that certain *particular* laws are illegitimate. But in that case, wouldn't the *punishment* under those *particular* laws also be illegitimate? What rationale yields the result that a law is unjust, yet punishments under that same law are just? Or that one has no obligation to obey the law, but one has an obligation to seek punishment for not obeying?

As a side note, there is a practical, propagandistic reason for civil disobedients to accept punishment: it communicates to the state and others that one's moral conviction is stronger than the fear that the state hopes to induce with its threats of punishment. Activists who hope to change society must weigh that consideration against the consideration that the state's punishments may physically prevent them from engaging in any further protest activities. Be that as it may, the philosophical point to make is that, just as there is no obligation to obey an unjust law, there is also no obligation to submit to unjust punishments.

6.5 May Everyone Do Whatever They Want?

The views advanced in the preceding sections, I have found, are easily misconstrued. It is common for people to assume that I am saying it is permissible to break the law (or nullify the law if you are a juror, refuse to enforce the law if you are a police officer, judge, or prosecutor, etc.) *whenever you want*, or whenever *you think* the law is wrong (regardless of whether your belief is at all reasonable or correct). And, of course, that is not what I am saying. That would, indeed, be a dumb view, which no one holds.

I am saying that it is permissible to violate the law (etc.) when the law *is unjust*. This does not entail that anyone may violate the law whenever they want, since it's not the case that the law is unjust whenever you *want* to violate it. It's also not the case that the law is unjust whenever *you think* that it is. You can be mistaken. If your beliefs are incorrect and you plan your actions based on those incorrect beliefs, then you may also wind up performing morally unjustified actions.

To illustrate my view, it may be useful to compare it to extremely widely held views about other types of actions. For instance, nearly everyone agrees that it is sometimes morally permissible to lie. Most of the time, of course, you shouldn't lie, but *sometimes* you should. I don't have a complete list of all the conditions in which lying is permissible. But I think that it is usually permissible to lie to prevent some *much worse* outcome from happening; for instance, you may tell a lie to prevent a murderer from finding his intended victim. Now, notice that this view does not entail that it is permissible to lie *whenever you want to*, or even that it is permissible to lie whenever *you think* (rationally or irrationally) that doing so would prevent a much worse outcome, or any similarly dumb thing. No one would make those mistakes. Similarly, then, we should not make the mistake of thinking that it is permissible to break the law whenever you want to or even whenever you think the law is unjust.

Notice also that the fact that I cannot give a complete algorithm for deciding in all cases whether lying is permissible does not mean that lying is either always wrong or always okay. Similarly, the fact that I do not have a complete algorithm for deciding in all cases whether breaking the law is permissible does not mean that breaking the law is either always wrong or always okay.

Another misunderstanding that sometimes occurs is that people think I am making claims about what someone's "job" is – for instance, that "it is a police officer's job to evaluate the justice of the laws." And, again, I am certainly not saying that. I agree that that is not the police officer's job – just as it is not the job of a Mafia hit man to evaluate the morality of murder. That is, neither of these people is being paid to exercise moral judgment, nor is the exercise of moral judgment part of either person's assigned role in the institution they belong to. I think, however, that questions about what one's job is are morally irrelevant in the present context; considerations about one's job description do nothing to excuse unjustly hurting other people.

7 Conclusion

The common notion of political authority places the state *above* other agents in a moral sense, granting the state a right to issue commands to everyone else and imposing obligations on everyone else to obey. This authority is held to be largely *content independent*, meaning that the reason for obeying particular laws, as well as the justification for imposing them, is simply that they are the commands of the government – they need not be the objectively correct rules by any independent standard. It is said that we are bound to obey the law, and government agents are bound to enforce it, even when it is a bad law.

If the state really has this kind of special moral status, it seems that there must be some explanation and justification for why that is the case. The most common accounts, however, fall flat. Some say, for instance, that the state's authority is established by a "contract" between the state and its citizens. There are a number of problems with this theory, beginning with the fact that we never actually signed such a contract, nor even verbally stated our acceptance of it. Contracts are supposed to be voluntary, but this "contract" is imposed upon one even if one explicitly states that one does not agree, even if one refrains from using government services, and even if one refrains from participating in the political process. The only effective method of avoiding subjection to government is to move to Antarctica. But it is not, in general, reasonable to declare that another person has "agreed" to obey your will simply because they are remaining on their own property rather than moving to Antarctica. Contracts are also supposed to involve mutual obligations. But in this case, the government does not, in fact, recognize any obligation to protect individuals, nor to provide any other services for any individual citizen. In standard contract doctrine, these problems would void any claim of a contractual obligation on the part of citizens.

Some philosophers appeal to a *hypothetical* social contract that we allegedly *would* have signed on to if we were deliberating about it in ideal conditions. But there is no reason to think that everyone would, in fact, agree on any substantive principles. Nor is there any reason to think that a purely hypothetical agreement is morally binding. Some thinkers say that the hypothetical agreement simply shows what is fair or reasonable. But in general, the fact that some proposed contract is fair or reasonable does not make it obligatory to follow it, nor permissible to forcibly impose it, if the agreement has not *in fact* been accepted.

Many people appeal to the democratic process for some kind of legitimation of the state. However, the fact that a majority of people wish to do something does not, in general, render the action permissible if it was not permissible to begin with – a majority may not legitimately decide to violate the rights of a minority. Though democracy might treat people as equals in some sense, this is not the sense that is morally important. The sense in which we are obligated to treat one another as equals is that of *respecting the equal rights* of all individuals – not that of giving everyone an equal say in deciding who shall forcibly impose their will on everyone else.

Finally, some say that the government may forcibly impose laws on people because this is necessary to maintain general social order, which is essential for any of us to have decent lives. However, this rationale could only justify the government in imposing laws that (i) are aimed at maintaining social order and (ii) are objectively *correct* and not, e.g., useless or counterproductive. Thus, we cannot justify a *content-independent* authority. Furthermore, only a very small fraction of government activities could be thought to satisfy both conditions (i) and (ii).

The best explanation for the failure of the leading accounts of authority is this: there is no authority. It is a moral illusion. Everyone is under the same moral constraints, regardless of what kind of uniform they wear or what organization they work for.

This leads to some highly revisionary political views. It implies that the state may only use coercion in circumstances and for purposes that would justify the use of coercion by ordinary agents. Given common-sense morality, this would essentially limit the legitimate laws to those that protect the rights of individuals against criminals and foreign invaders – the functions of the "minimal state." When the law goes beyond what is necessary to provide social order and protect the rights of individuals, it is ethically permissible for individuals to disregard the law – and it is ethically *impermissible* for government agents to enforce that law. Individuals who violate such illegitimate laws are under no obligation to accept punishment since any such punishment is equally illegitimate. Citizens who are asked to help implement the laws by serving on juries should also refuse to enforce unjust laws.

This does not mean that individuals are free to do whatever they *want* or whatever they *believe* to be appropriate. There are moral constraints independent of the law – for example, one may not rob, kill, attack, or defraud other individuals. This is true independent of the law, so, of course, one should not violate the laws against murder, theft, and so on. It is only the morally illegitimate laws, those that go beyond the functions of the minimal state, that are appropriately disregarded.

References

Achen, Christopher H. and Larry Bartels. 2016. *Democracy for Realists: Why Elections Do Not Produce Responsive Government*. Princeton, NJ: Princeton University Press.

Adams, John. 1771. *Diary 16, 10 January 1771–28 November 1772*. Retrieved April 14, 2020 from www.masshist.org/digitaladams/archive/doc?id=D16.

Brennan, Jason. 2016. *Against Democracy*. Princeton, NJ: Princeton University Press.

Brooks, Ned (reporter). 1965, March 28. "Meet The Press: Martin Luther King, Jr. on the Selma March" (television series episode), *Meet the Press*. NBC Universal Media. Retrieved April 14, 2020 from https://archives.nbclearn.com/portal/site/k-12/browse/?cuecard=48756.

Caplan, Bryan. 2007. *The Myth of the Rational Voter*. Princeton, NJ: Princeton University Press.

Christiano, Thomas. 2008. *The Constitution of Equality: Democratic Authority and Its Limits*. Oxford: Oxford University Press.

Cohen, Joshua. 1989. "Deliberation and Democratic Legitimacy", pp. 17–34 in *The Good Polity*, ed. Alan Hamlin and Phillip Petit. New York: Blackwell.

Friedman, David. 1989. *The Machinery of Freedom*. LaSalle, IL: Open Court.

Habermas, Jürgen. 2002. "Deliberative Politics", pp. 107–125 in *Democracy*, ed. David Estlund. Malden, MA: Blackwell.

Hamilton, Alexander. 1788. "The Judiciary Continued in Relation to Trial by Jury", *Federalist* No. 83. Retrieved April 14, 2020 from www.congress.gov/resources/display/content/The+Federalist+Papers.

Hobbes, Thomas. [1651] 1996. *Leviathan*, ed. Richard Tuck. Cambridge: Cambridge University Press.

Huemer, Michael. 2013. *The Problem of Political Authority*. New York: Palgrave Macmillan.

Huemer, Michael. 2018. "The Duty to Disregard the Law", *Criminal Law and Philosophy* 12: 1–18.

Hume, David. [1777] 1987. "Of the Original Contract", pp. 465–487 in *Essays, Moral, Political, and Literary*. Indianapolis, IN: Liberty Fund.

Jefferson, Thomas. 1789, July 11. *Letter to Thomas Paine*. Retrieved April 14, 2020 from https://founders.archives.gov/documents/Jefferson/01-15-02-0259.

Klosko, George. 2005. *Political Obligations*. Oxford: Oxford University Press.

Nagel, Thomas. 1991. *Equality and Partiality*. New York: Oxford University Press.

Rawls, John. 1999. *A Theory of Justice*, revised ed. Cambridge, MA: Harvard University Press.

Rawls, John. 2005. *Political Liberalism*, expanded ed. New York: Columbia University Press.

Rothbard, Murray. 1978. *For a New Liberty*. Lanham, MD: University Press of America.

Scanlon, Thomas M. 1998. *What We Owe to Each Other*. Cambridge, MA: Harvard University Press.

Simmons, A. John. 1979. *Moral Principles and Political Obligation*. Princeton, NJ: Princeton University Press.

Stringham, Edward P., ed. 2007. *Anarchy and the Law: The Political Economy of Choice*. New Brunswick, NJ: Transaction Publishers.

United States Sentencing Commission. 2018, November 1. *Guidelines Manual*. Retrieved from www.ussc.gov/guidelines/.

Chapter 2

Rights, Respect, and Equality
The Basis of Authority

Daniel Layman

Contents

I The Problem of Political Authority

Governments have authority to the extent that they have a right to rule their citizens and those citizens have a duty to obey. But do any actual governments possess authority? Obviously, governments have power, and plenty of it; they can and do pass laws and force people to obey them. But why is that power rightful, and why do citizens have a moral duty, as opposed to merely reasons of fear or prudence, to obey?

In the previous chapter, my coauthor, Michael Huemer, argues that there has never been any genuine political authority and that none is likely ever to arise. This, in turn, means that the billions of people around the world who believe in political authority are suffering from a kind of mass delusion. Huemer seeks to awaken

DOI: 10.4324/9780429328046-4

us from our dogmatic slumbers and help us see clearly for the first time the real, waking world of individual rights and duties without any special role for the state. I am going to defend the contrary position. Genuine political authority, I believe, is very much a live possibility in our social world. Indeed, many (but not all) states possess genuine authority to a very considerable degree. But before I launch into my solution to the problem of political authority, we need to get clearer on what exactly that problem is – and why it is a problem at all.

Why is there, in addition to a question of political authority, a problem of political authority? The question of political authority is just what it sounds like: Do any governments (or, perhaps, *could* any governments) have political authority? Following Huemer, I take political authority to be a composite of two distinct moral components: *political legitimacy* – the right of the state to issue and enforce the law – and *political obligation* – citizens' duty to obey the state. The question of political authority comprises two narrower questions. First, what conditions do states need to meet to have authority? Second, which states, if any, meet those conditions? Nothing further in particular needs to be the case for the question of political authority to make sense, simply as a question. After all, people can (and do) ask boring questions, so there would be a question of political authority even if it had an obvious answer. The question of authority emerges as the *problem* of authority only to the extent that we think that there is something difficult, vexing, or nonobvious about it. More specifically, the question of political authority emerges as the problem of political authority only when we begin to suspect that there is good reason to doubt that it has the answer that most people assume that it has. Nearly everyone who has grown up within an established nation-state – which is to say, nearly everyone – will notice that most of the institutions of governance, education, commerce, and even family and religion within which they live their lives operate on the tacit or explicit assumption that the government is authoritative. But once we start to reflect on the question of political authority, it quickly begins to look like a serious problem.

Huemer draws out the intuition that there is a problem of political authority by asking us to consider cases of private persons doing things that governments characteristically do. He invites us to imagine a vigilante who takes it upon herself to round up local vandals, punish them, and then demand payment from the rest of her neighborhood to fund her antivandalism efforts. Most of us, he correctly notes, would judge that even if the vigilante was justified in rounding up and punishing the vandals (and this is questionable), none of us has any duty to pay her, and she has no right to force us to pay. But doesn't the government lock people up for harmful behavior and then tax its citizens to support its efforts? If it is clearly wrong for the vigilante to behave in this way, why isn't it also wrong when the government does so?

Huemer is right to think that cases like that of the vigilante help us see that the idea of political authority is much more problematic than we often suppose. But although such cases bring the problem of political authority forcefully to our attention, they do not suffice to spell out the full content of the problem. To understand not just *that* political authority is problematic but also *why* it is problematic, we need to dig deeper. In particular, we need to ask ourselves why the vigilante's behavior is unacceptable. Once we have answered this question, we will be able to establish criteria that governments must meet to have an acceptable moral relationship with their citizens. Establishing such criteria will not, of course, suffice to establish that any governments meet them; anarchism, or the absence of political authority, will still be very much on the table. Nevertheless, establishing them will help us structure our search for an adequate account of how that conclusion might be avoided.

Despite officially declining to pursue the problem of political authority beyond the observation that people like the vigilante behave wrongly, Huemer does gesture toward a compelling account of what goes morally wrong in the vigilante case: the vigilante's behavior is incompatible with people's *equal rights*. He writes: "It is plausible that we are obligated to treat all people as equals in the sense of recognizing *the same rights* for all people." Moreover: "The Problem of Political Authority arises in the first place because the government is engaged in activities that would be considered wrongful, indeed as violations of individual rights, if anyone else were to do them." Huemer's language here calls to mind the words of John Locke, whose ill-fated consent theory of political authority you encountered in the previous chapter. According to Locke, the basic moral condition of adult human beings is "a state . . . of equality, wherein all the power and jurisdiction is reciprocal, no one having more than another."[1] If all people have the same rights, then why are people who work for the government entitled to behave as though they have special rights?

All of this strikes me as exactly correct; the vigilante's actions are unacceptable because they are in tension with our equal rights. Consequently, in order for governments' relationships with their citizens to be any more acceptable than the vigilante's relationship to her victims, governments must – somehow – respect citizens' equal rights even while commanding them and compelling their obedience. In short, the problem of political authority is the problem of how equal rights for all are compatible with both (a) legitimate government power to issue and enforce commands and (b) obligations on the part of citizens to obey government commands, not just in some tightly circumscribed domain of activity, but across most dimensions of life.

In what remains, I will argue that governments have authority to the extent that, subject to an appropriately democratic procedure, they issue and enforce law and policy necessary for people to relate to one another as equal rights-holders. My account will be, broadly speaking, Kantian. This is not because Immanuel Kant has any special authority (he doesn't) or because he was always right (he wasn't), but because his approach to political authority is correct, at least in its essentials. However, since my goal here is to get political authority right rather than to get Kant right, I will frequently and freely depart from Kant's opinions. Indeed, certain portions of my argument draw on other figures (Locke, for instance) to an extent that Kant would likely have found highly objectionable. Moreover, I will turn to contemporary philosophers working in a Kantian vein whenever their texts strike me as more perspicuous than Kant's own.

Aside: Immanuel Kant (1724–1804)

Kant's political philosophy, which he sets out in his *Metaphysics of Morals*, is less well known than his theory of knowledge, in which he synthesizes elements of empiricism and rationalism, and his moral philosophy, in which he elaborates the idea of a moral law derived from pure practical reason. Nevertheless,

---

1. Locke 1988, § 4.

it occupies a very important place in the history of liberalism, as it accommodates the rights-based individualism of
natural law thinkers such as Locke to the highly developed
republicanism of eighteenth-century continental philosophers
such as Rousseau. Despite being one of the earliest writers on
what we would now call global governance, Kant apparently
never traveled more than 100 miles from the Prussian town of
Königsberg (now the Russian city of Kaliningrad)!

In the course of my argument, I will need to show that two
things are true of both legitimacy and obligation – which
together constitute authority – within democratic states. First,
I will need to show that the authority of such states is **content
independent,** or valid regardless of the particular laws that they
issue. As Huemer rightly recognizes in Chapter 1, I do not need
to show that authority is totally content independent, or that
governments have authority no matter what they do. Such a
view would be very implausible, and I do not mean to defend it.
Nevertheless, I do need to show that, within a significant range
of law and policy, citizens are obligated to do what the government tells them to do because the government has told them
to do it. Second, I need to show that a government's authority
is **particular** to the people who live under it. If my theory ends
up entailing that Americans are obligated to obey the government of Belize (or vice versa), something will have gone terribly
wrong.

With these preliminaries complete, it is time to dive in. Since the
whole account on offer here turns on rights, we will do well to
begin by getting clear on what they are, why they matter, and how
they can be violated.

2 Rights

Let's begin with a distinction between two senses in which someone might be said to have a right.[2] One sense in which someone
might have a right to do something is merely to be permitted to

---

2. Hohfeld 1923.

do it. In this sense, I have a right to pick up a quarter I encounter on the sidewalk as I walk by. If I decide to pick up the quarter and do so, a person ten feet behind me, whose liberties we may suppose are the same as mine and who would have liked to pick it up for herself, has no grounds to complain. This sort of right is a **permission right**. In other cases, though, people have rights that are not mere liberties but rather liberties accompanied by claims to exercise them. If I have a right to the quarter in this sense, I have standing to insist that others leave the quarter – *my* quarter – alone and maybe even to force them to do so. Such **claim rights** are what concern me here.

Why should we think that we have any rights? After all, to say that someone has a right is to say something quite specific and demanding. It is not merely to say that that person has a strong reason to do or possess something, or even that it is extremely important from a moral point of view that she do or possess it. On the contrary, to attribute a right to someone is to say that she is "a small-scale sovereign" within the right's sphere: what she decides within that sphere stands authoritatively, just because she decided it.[3] So, for instance, if I have a right to the quarter from our previous example, I get to possess it – or spend it, or throw it into a river, or press it into a necklace charm, or whatever – for any reason or no reason at all. And if someone tries to take it from me without permission, I have standing to object and perhaps even to resist. Why admit moral entities like this into our moral framework? Why not just focus on the relative goodness or importance of various actions and states of affairs and dispense with rights?

One of the most famous answers to this question (and one of the best) is that it is important not just that our interests be furthered, but also that we have standing to claim certain interests against others, in our own voice and on our own authority, because we are moral equals who should respect one another as such.[4] A significant difference between saying "It's really important that my bodily integrity not be violated" and "I have a right to bodily integrity" is that only the latter entails standing to say to actual or prospective

---

3. Hart 1982, p. 183.
4. Feinberg 1970.

bodily invaders: You. Step off. I insist.[5] By claiming our own rights and respecting others' rights, we practice our moral equality and independence. As we will later discuss, the fundamental rights recognized by such enlightenment liberals as Locke and Kant are precisely those that make it possible for us to relate to one another in this way.

We now have a sense of what rights are and why they matter. Now let's consider what it takes for rights to suffer violation. All rights theorists agree that a person's right counts as violated by **invasion** or active interference. If, for instance, I have a right to my quarter, you violate my right if you attempt to take it or otherwise impede my use of it. But invasion is not the only source of rights violation. Since the moral point of rights is to establish spheres of micro-sovereignty among individuals, rights can also be violated by other people's arbitrary power over rights holders even if that power goes unused. As Bas van der Vossen puts the point: "Non-subjection is an implication of our natural rights, requiring that our ability to enjoy those rights doesn't depend on others' actions."[6] This is why Locke, perhaps the rights theorist par excellence, builds freedom from arbitrary power into his definition of individual freedom:

> All men are naturally in . . . a state of perfect freedom to order their actions, and dispose of their possessions and persons, as they think fit, within the bounds of the law of nature, without asking leave, or depending upon the will of any other man.[7]

Someone who can use her rights – in Locke's language, "dispose of their possessions and persons" – but only by "depending on the will of [another] man" is not free. Freedom from arbitrary power within rights constitutes rightful freedom no less than freedom from invasion does. Let's call violation of rights by

---

5. Stephen Darwall calls the "you" stance we take towards others when we assert our rights the "second-person standpoint" (Darwall 2006). It is this standpoint that makes possible our moral practices of claiming and holding accountable as opposed to merely describing what is good or bad, better or worse.
6. Van der Vossen 2020, pp. 7–8.
7. Locke 1988, § 4.

arbitrary power "rights **vitiation**" to distinguish it from rights invasion.[8]

A nonpolitical example will help to clarify the idea of rights vitiation. Most people would agree that college students have certain rights against their professors concerning the quality and fairness of professors' teaching and evaluation. Students have a right, for instance, not to be treated differently based on their race, gender, sexuality, or political beliefs, to have their (reasonable) questions answered in a timely manner, and not to be examined on any material that hasn't been covered. Now, suppose that at Political Philosophy University (PPU), professors all do, in fact, respect their students' rights. However, PPU has an unusual institutional structure: unlike most colleges of which I'm aware, PPU lacks institutions for securing students' rights. Although professors at PPU treat students equally, answer reasonable questions, and grade fairly, PPU has no procedures of any kind for holding professors accountable. Imagine now that upon discovering this fact about PPU, Jana, a student there, vents to a friend at another college: "We don't have any rights here!" If her friend replied, "Yes you do! You have moral claims, and no one ever invades them," Jana would rightly judge that her friend had missed the point. "Sure," she would say, "we have rights in the sense that we have moral claims, but due to the total lack of accountability here, they are meaningless. They count for nothing because they don't secure our standing within those claims' spheres, which is the whole point of rights." Jana's rights as a student might not be invaded, but they are vitiated – and so violated – anyway.

In the next section, I am going to argue that without government, our rights necessarily suffer vitiation even if they don't suffer invasion – although invasion is very much on the table under such circumstances. This means that for us to live freely as equal holders of unviolated rights, we must live within a state that passes, enforces, and adjudicates law to which all are accountable. States have a right to rule not despite our individual rights but on account of them.

---

8. I borrow (with some alteration) the language of vitiation and invasion from Philip Pettit 2012, pp. 35–49.

3   Self-Government and Property

Rights theorists often disagree about the content of rights despite agreeing that individual rights are both real and fundamentally important. For instance, Lysander Spooner's **anarcho-capitalism**[9] – the view that we should replace states, which lack authority, with pure capitalism – and John Rawls's **social democracy** – a leftwing form of liberalism in which property is subject to democratic control – both plausibly count as rights theories.[10] Nevertheless, the very idea of rights – or, at least, of *equal* rights – entails what we may call a **right of self-government**, or **self-government** for short. Anna Stilz explains that self-government

> gives us the title to do anything to other people that we may do to them without actually diminishing their freedom as independence, like simply communicating our thoughts to them: it thus grounds rights to freedom of speech and thought. Second, it gives us title to insist that we not be bound by any restrictions to freedom that are not reciprocal restrictions, that do not bind other people in the same way: it justifies a right to equal treatment.[11]

Insofar as we are committed to the idea of equal basic rights at all, we are committed to self-government. After all, our claims against one another could hardly secure each of us an equal space of personal control without it. But few rights theorists are content to stop there. Most philosophers who accept self-government argue that it entails further rights of **property**. Unlike self-government, which extends only to each person's body and mind, property rights apply to portions of the world around us. Although philosophers who accept the move from self-government to property disagree

---

9. According to Spooner, natural rights, among which property rights occupy a seat of the highest privilege, exist from eternity in a fully determinate form that we may learn as a kind of "science" (Spooner 1882).
10. Rawls argues that the "basic rights"—or rights that may not be traded off for other kinds of goods—include all and only those necessary for citizens to develop adequately their two "moral powers": a sense of justice and a conception of the good. These basic rights notably include personal property rights but not productive property rights. (Rawls 2005, Lecture VIII)
11. Stilz 2009, p. 36.

about how people come to hold property and how much each person may hold, they agree that self-government in a material world like ours is impossible without property. John Simmons explains: "Property is an indispensable condition of self-government. Property does not . . . just ensure survival; it is also the security for our freedom, protecting us against dependence on the will of others and the subservience to them that this creates."[12] If I am to put self-government to work in pursuit of my projects, I am going to need to control some portion of the extra-personal world. Moreover, if I am to do so on terms that answer to the idea of *equal* self-government, I am going to need to control some portion of the world on my own terms, without subjection to others' arbitrary power or discretion. And this, of course, is just to say that I must have standing to claim some portion of the external world as my right. Hence, if there is self-government, there must be property as well. Stilz, glossing Kant, complements Simmons's reasoning:

> In order to freely pursue any minimally sophisticated project, we need more than simply the right to use objects while we are physically holding them. Imagine, for example, that I want to paint a landscape. It is clearly insufficient for me to achieve this goal that I possess the use right to dispose of paint, brushes, and canvas without fear of assault by others while I am holding them. For it is consistent with such a right that as soon as I put down the materials, someone else could come in and undo what I have done. To pursue any sophisticated goal, then, we have to be capable of making objects ours, by annexing them to our own rightful private sphere in the external world. Property rights are in this way essential conditions of agents' autonomy.[13]

Self-Government, then, entails property. However, it doesn't entail any particular allotment of property, at least not without some additional steps in the argument. For even if we grant self-government and accept property as its consequence, we still don't know who owns what or even how this question might be settled. Perhaps the most famous answer comes from Locke. According to Locke, people create property rights in particular portions of

---

12. Simmons 1992, p. 274.
13. Stilz 2009, p. 39.

the physical world by *working* on particular portions of the physical world. Locke reasons that since we have exclusive rights to our own bodies and bodily actions, we must own parts of the physical world that we "mix" with our labor.[14] Of course, Locke does not mean to claim that people can come to own anything at all by mixing their labor with it. To the contrary, he places two relevant restrictions (in addition to a theologically grounded rule about waste, which we may ignore here) on private appropriation.[15] First, and most obviously, no one can acquire another person's property by laboring on it, as that would run contrary to the whole point of property, which is to extend the protections of self-government into the shared world. Second, people must restrict their appropriation so that there is "enough, and as good left in common for others."[16] Following recent scholarship, we may call this second restriction the **Lockean proviso** on property. By observing the proviso, an appropriator "leaves [others] free to appropriate a similar share within which to actualize their own right of self-government."[17]

Aside: John Locke (1632–1704)

In the context of political authority, the English philosopher Locke is best known for his consent theory. But Locke's doctrine of consent is only one piece of a comprehensive political theory that he composed during the early-to-mid 1680s to pave the way for the "Glorious Revolution" of 1688, which deposed Charles II and enthroned William of Orange and his wife, Mary. The core of that theory – which also sets out a well-known account of private property – is the idea that all persons are naturally in a moral position to "order their actions, and dispose of their possessions and persons, as they think fit, within the bounds of the law of nature, without asking leave, or depending upon the will of any other man" (*Second Treatise* 4).

---

14. Locke 1988, § 27.
15. Locke holds that it is impermissible to take so much that resources "spoil," or go to waste before the appropriator can put them to use. This is because "nothing was made by God for man to spoil or destroy" (Locke 1988, § 31).
16. Locke 1988, § 27.
17. Stilz 2009, p. 35.

So far, we have seen how the Lockean and the Kantian move in lockstep from equal rights to self-government to property. But we have now reached the point at which they diverge. Whereas the Lockean holds that freedom within equal rights is possible (albeit unlikely) without government, the Kantian insists that where there is no public power, people cannot live together in a way that is compatible with their rights. This is because any **state of nature** – that is, any state of affairs without government – is necessarily plagued by three defects that vitiate equal rights.[18] Governments are legitimate, and their citizens have obligations to them, insofar as they correct these defects, thereby making rightful relationships possible. Since Kantian political obligation depends on Kantian legitimacy, I will begin with the latter before turning to the former.

4   Legitimacy I: Three State of Nature Defects

As we saw earlier, Locke holds that individuals extend self-government into the world by "joining" their labor or action to the objects on which they labor, thereby turning them into private property. There is clearly something right about Locke's insight here; self-government for embodied agents requires the government of external things as well, so self-governors must have standing to claim portions of the external world as their own. The trouble, though, is that the conceptual connection that exists between self-government and property, tight and compelling though it is, fails to determine which pieces of the external world people may claim as property. Moreover, simply leaning on the metaphor of joining labor to bits of the world will not suffice to bridge this conceptual gap. To make progress, we will need additional conceptual resources beyond those Locke offers.[19]

---

18. I here agree with Ripstein 2009 that there are three genuinely distinct rights-oriented defects in the state of nature. For an argument that the judicial defect and the executive defect are not really distinct from the legislative defect, see Christmas 2021.

19. It is important to note that the worry about appropriation I am pursuing here is not that people may not unilaterally create obligations for other people by seizing pieces of the world as they see fit. As Bas van der Vossen has shown, there is no reason why Lockean appropriation cannot be understood in terms of individuals activating preexisting conditional rights that assign property rights in resources to whatever person meets preexisting action conditions (Van der Vossen 2015). The present concern is not that Lockean appropriation is objectionably unilateral but rather that, unilaterally established or not, the boundaries of those rights are indeterminate without public legal authority.

Consider Locke's example of a person acquiring a property right in a hare that she is hunting. According to Locke, there is no need for the hunter to catch the hare or even touch it for it to become her property.[20] This judgment fits well with the idea that appropriation amounts to incorporating elements of the world into one's action and, consequently, one's self-government; the action of pursuit, after all, is no less real for being unsuccessful. Nonetheless, it fails to establish how far the hunter's right extends, and why. Imagine that our hunter believes (correctly) that the hare she is chasing is leading her to a whole field full of hares that she intends to capture upon arrival. Does she, therefore, own all the hares as soon as she gives chase to the first one? What about the field itself, assuming she has an intention to use it for something (as a breeding ground for all the hares, perhaps)? And if so, where are the boundaries of the field? As long as there is nothing in play but individuals and their purposes, it isn't clear how to answer these questions and others like them. What self-governing individuals need to acquire determinate property rights is a set of rules that supplements the general right to control portions of the extra-personal world with laws establishing who gets what, when. The absence of any such set of rules in the state of nature is the first of our three defects: the **legislative defect**.[21]

Next, there is the **judicial defect**. Even if (contrary to fact) the state of nature had determinate property rules, there would still be the matter of assessing how particular actions and states of affairs relate to them, especially in the face of disagreement. Locke, who thinks (contrary to what I have just argued) that property rights are determinate in the state of nature, recognizes this problem: "the inconveniencies of the state of nature . . . must certainly be great, where men may be judges in their own case."[22] In the state of nature, parties who disagree about how to apply the rules governing rights to particular cases must ultimately "appeal to heaven" – that is, fight it out.[23] Thus, without a judicial power to settle disputes on everyone's behalf, whether and how disagreements about how to apply rules governing rights find (nonviolent) resolution would hinge entirely on the personalities, dispositions, and abilities of the people who happen to be involved.

20. Locke 1988, § 30.
21. Kant 1996, 6:258.
22. Locke 1988, § 13.
23. Locke 1988, § 21.

Finally, even if the state of nature didn't suffer from the first two defects, life therein would still suffer from a problem of assurance.[24] In order for law and adjudication to provide a framework in which individuals can put their rights to work in constructing and pursuing their plans, people need to be able to rely on a public, commonly known mechanism of enforcement. The problematic absence of any such mechanism in the state of nature is its **executive defect**.

Locke was no less aware of the executive defect than the judicial defect: "The law of nature would, as all other laws that concern men in this world be in vain, if there were nobody that in the state of nature had a power to execute that law, and thereby preserve the innocent and restrain offenders."[25] In order to head off this threat, he introduces a universal executive right, according to which "by the law of nature every man hath . . . a power to punish offences against it, as he soberly judges the case to require."[26] Locke admits that this is likely to strike his readers as a "strange doctrine."[27] But he insists that two compelling grounds together leave us little choice but to accept it. First, any law, whether natural or artificial, can only be "in vain" – that is, pointless – unless it includes a structure of enforcement along with its prescriptions.[28] For without such a structure of enforcement, people cannot count on others' accountability under the law, which in turn means that rights included in the law cannot play their characteristic role of making rights-holders "small-scale sovereigns" within their scope. Second, since we are all morally equal self-governors, it is out of the question for anyone to hold a right to enforce the law of nature unless everyone does.

It might seem that if Locke is right about the natural executive right, there is no executive defect after all since everyone in the state of nature may execute the law. This is not the case, though. For even if everyone did hold such a right (which, with all due respect to Locke, we must admit is far from obvious), everyone would have to decide on the means and severity of enforcement by appeal to

---

24. Kant 1996, 6:256.
25. Locke 1988, § 7.
26. Locke 1988, § 9.
27. Locke 1988, § 9.
28. Locke 1988, § 7.

nothing beyond her "own calm reason and conscience."[29] Locke himself is unimpressed with the prospects of such an enforcement regime. He writes:

> IF man in the state of nature be so free, as has been said; if he be absolute lord of his own person and possessions, equal to the greatest, and subject to no body, why will he part with his freedom? . . . To which it is obvious to answer, that though in the state of nature he hath such a right, yet the enjoyment of it is very uncertain, and constantly exposed to the invasion of others: for all being kings as much as he, every man his equal, and the greater part no strict observers of equity and justice, the enjoyment of the property he has in this state is very unsafe, very unsecure.[30]

This is why "mankind, notwithstanding all the privileges of the state of nature, being but in an ill condition, while they remain in it, are quickly driven into society" (II, 127). But suppose that someone is lucky enough to be surrounded by judicious and high-minded people who always enforce the natural law correctly. Would such a person's freedom still suffer on account of the executive defect? Surely, such a lucky person's freedom would still suffer precisely because her ability to act successfully within her rights turns on nothing but other people's preferences and dispositions. Luck of the draw with respect to the preferences and dispositions of other people is no genuine assurance at all, let alone assurance sufficient for freedom within rights.

5   Legitimacy II: Government Is Necessary to Remedy the State of Nature's Defects

As we observed earlier, arbitrary power within rights violates rights by vitiating them, even without interference. This is because arbitrary power within rights undermines the point of rights, which is to define and protect spheres of action and choice within which individuals are, in Hart's memorable phrase, "small-scale sovereigns."

---

29. Locke 1988, § 8.
30. Locke 1988, § 123.

When one's rights remain free from interference only because that suits some unaccountable person, those rights are violated, even though no one has invaded them. For under such circumstances, it is the unaccountable person rather than the rights-holder who, in fact, enjoys small-scale sovereignty within the scope of the relevant rights. Each of the three defects of the state of nature subjects self-government and property to arbitrary power and so to violation. For people to enjoy their rights unviolated, they must share an institutional framework that corrects these defects. For reasons I will now elaborate over the next several sections, that framework must be a governmental framework. By establishing this much, we will have shown that government, far from violating citizens' rights, is a necessary condition of citizens' enjoying their rights at all. And since the problem of legitimacy is the problem of how governments can rule without violating rights, we will have arrived at an account of political legitimacy as well.

Each of the three defects we considered in the last section is defective insofar as it subjects rights to arbitrary power in its own way. The legislative defect subjects rights to arbitrary power because settling property boundaries can, in the absence of determinate legal boundaries, turn on nothing more than the judgments and preferences of those best able to enforce their wills. Similarly, the judicial defect subjects rights to arbitrary power insofar as it makes the application of rights to particular cases turn on nothing more than the judgments and preferences of those best able to enforce their wills. And, finally, the executive defect subjects rights to arbitrary power – and would do so even in the absence of the legislative and judicial defects – insofar as it makes rights enforcement turn on nothing more than the judgments and preferences of those best able to enforce their wills.

One way to describe the single conceptual thread that conjoins all three defects is that each one subjects some dimension of freedom within rights to others' unilateral wills. To the extent that rights are indeterminate, fail to be justiciable, or lack assurance, people may simply fill in the leftover space by exercising their own wills as they see fit. Kant argues that what people need to live together in a condition of right is a "unified" will.[31] This approach, however,

---

31. Kant 1996, 6:314.

strikes me as both confused and unnecessary. It is confused because it is not at all obvious what it might mean for some large plurality of people to have a common will. Insofar as this idea makes sense at all, it seems to presuppose that a large, diverse group of people can become a collective agent by associating politically.[32] There is a great deal of debate about what it takes for groups to constitute collective agents, and it is controversial (to say the least) whether even the best democracies make the cut. It would, therefore, be risky business to put much theoretical weight on so shaky a proposition.[33] Happily, there is no need to do so. For what the three state-of-nature defects demand is not the *presence* of some new, collective kind of will but rather the *absence* of unilateral (and so arbitrary) power over others' rights. To live freely within their rights, people need to design and occupy institutions that remove legislation, enforcement, and adjudication from individual judgment and subject them to institutions that are equally in force for, and accountable to, all community members alike.[34]

At this point, you probably see the conclusion I'm driving at: the institutions necessary to remove the kind of unilateral power that necessarily vitiates rights in the state of nature are state institutions. But to make good on this claim, it is necessary to address two very important (and closely related) questions.

First: Why isn't government just one more arbitrary power, like Huemer's vigilante? Even if a government has highly complex judicial, executive, and legislative institutions, complete with rigorous internal checks and balances, why isn't it still an arbitrary agent? Shouldn't consent (which actual governments surely lack) be

---

32. For an example of an account of legitimacy that does turn on group agency, see Applbaum 2019.

33. According to Christian List's and Philip Pettit's influential account of group agency, group agents must have "representational states, motivational states, and a capacity to process them and to act on that basis in the manner of an agent" (List and Pettit 2011, p. 32). Although it may well be possible for democratic political communities to meet this standard, I will not assume as much here.

34. It is important to note that my argument does not turn on the claim that rights are necessarily indeterminate in the state of nature, a claim that receives extended criticism in Christmas 2021. Rather, my claim will be that without the state, rights cannot be rendered determinate *in a way that adequately secures basic equal accountability*.

necessary to transform arbitrary, unaccountable government power into nonarbitrary, accountable government power?

Second: Even if there is some reason to believe that government is not just one more arbitrary power, why couldn't other, nongovernmental agencies also avoid being arbitrary powers? Why couldn't private entities of various kinds – security firms, private courts, and so forth – remedy the three defects just as well as government? This question is especially pressing because Huemer has elsewhere argued at length that non-state actors can and should carry out the relatively few worthwhile state functions.[35]

My reply to the second question turns almost entirely on my answer to the first. The key claim that underwrites both answers is that the state must institute equal basic accountability to all citizens through democratic institutions. It will be useful to introduce our discussion of democracy by returning to Huemer's argument from the last chapter against the claim that democracy can ground political authority. According to Huemer, theorists who affirm political authority on democratic grounds argue as follows:

1. In a democratic society, the laws are supported by the majority of people.
2. If something is supported by the majority of people, then it is obligatory to go along with it, and it is permissible to forcibly impose it on everyone, including those who do not agree with it.
3. Therefore, in a democratic society, it is obligatory to obey the laws, and it is permissible to forcibly impose those laws on everyone.

According to Huemer, both premises 1 and 2 are false. Premise 1 is false because, in all modern states, law is both fantastically complex and largely authored by agencies rather than directly by legislatures. So, almost no one knows what the laws are, and even if people did know, the fact that agencies make most laws would belie the idea that they reflect the preferences of the majority. Premise 2 is false because it is simply untrue that there is any general moral rule to the effect that we are obligated to obey decisions that majorities support. If, for instance, a majority of people at dinner decided

---

35. Huemer 2013, Part II.

I had to pay, I would have no obligation to do so, and my fellow diners certainly wouldn't have any standing to make me do so.

I agree with Huemer. Both premises are false, so we had better not rely on them. Happily, the argument of this section is different in two very important ways from the one Huemer reconstructs. First, it will make no appeal to the idea that democracy secures majority support for particular laws. In place of this idea, I will develop the distinct concept of **equal basic accountability** within democratic institutions. Second, my appeal to democracy is not an appeal to some stand-alone moral principle about the authority of majoritarian decision-making. To the contrary, it is an appeal to the capacity of democratic institutions to subject power to equal basic accountability. When people are subject only to legal structures that manifest equal basic accountability to all who live under them, government power is nonarbitrary. And this, in turn, means that government power can correct the three defects that plague the state of nature without reproducing the arbitrary power that makes those defects so objectionable.

To get a grip on the idea of equal basic accountability, it will be useful to begin with the distinct but related idea of equally shared control. Philip Pettit has recently argued that in order for power relationships to be nonarbitrary, the person subject to power within the relationship must be in control of that power.[36] For example, if someone can determine capriciously whether I have access to my liquor cabinet, then she holds arbitrary power over me with respect to that access.[37] But if she has access to my liquor cabinet key only on terms, and for purposes, that I design and implement – say, for a period of three days to help me with my goal of cutting back on my drinking – then I am ultimately in control and her power is nonarbitrary. Pettit extends this principle of nonarbitrariness via control to his account of political legitimacy. Political power is legitimate, Pettit argues, just in case the people subject to it also control it. When this is the case, state power avoids being arbitrary and thus respects its citizens' freedom.

Of course, it is not possible for each individual to control the government as an individual might control a friend's power over

---

36. Pettit 2012, pp. 146–153.
37. Pettit 2012, p. 152.

her liquor cabinet. If an individual did hold such control, she would simply be a dictator and everyone would then need to worry about *her* arbitrary power. Pettit's suggestion is instead that government is legitimate only when all share equally in controlling the government through democratic procedures. In order for this shared control to be effective, it is necessary not only that each person has equal access to deliberation and voting – what we might call "front end" democratic control – but also that each person has equal access to the "back end" democratic control whereby citizens may contest government actions after the fact.[38] Government is legitimate only to the extent that it is subject to both of these dimensions of equal joint control.

Pettit is onto something very important here. For nonarbitrary power must be, in some sense, answerable to the people subject to it. Nevertheless, the control model of answerability faces two serious problems. Close attention to these problems will point the way to a more successful account of that relationship, one that turns on accountability rather than on control. The first problem is that no advanced political community is subject to control by its populace in any ordinary sense. Control can be understood as a function – that is, as a relationship between inputs to a system and outputs from that system. An agent enjoys control with respect to a system to the extent that outputs change only in accordance with her inputs. Thus, I am in control of withdrawals from my savings account, as money is withdrawn only at the times and in the amounts that I designate. Similarly, the Board of Trustees at my college controls tenure there, as faculty receive tenure only if the board decides that they should. It is perhaps tempting to think that "we the people" relate to the laws of our state in much the way that the board of trustees relates to tenure cases. But this simply is not so. Even if elected officials made all law directly, and if there were robust, powerful, and direct avenues of contestation available to all citizens, it would still be a stretch to say that we the people control the power of government. It would perhaps be plausible to say that we control some major sources of influence on that power, but that wouldn't be quite the same thing as controlling that power itself. In any event, and as Huemer effectively points out, agencies create and

---

38. Pettit 2012, Chapter 5.

enforce a great deal of law, and there is really no avenue by which citizens may contest what they do, at least not apart from voting for different politicians during the next election cycle. Moreover, these difficulties hold even if we ignore the myriad inequities of campaign finance, which I will discuss later. In short, the people do not control the government even under the best circumstances, let alone under the circumstances we face.

The second problem with the control model of legitimacy is that even if, contrary to fact, we the people were to control government power, it isn't clear why the power of the whole community wouldn't be arbitrary with respect to each individual member. On Pettit's hypothesis, it is control that makes the difference between arbitrary power and nonarbitrary power. But even if I have an equal share in the collective mechanism that controls the state, it isn't true that *I* control the state. Indeed, having an equal share in the community's control of the state doesn't mean that I control the state any more than the Board of Trustees' control of tenure means that any particular trustee controls tenure. One might reply that although individual citizens don't control the state, they do share equally in the community's control of the state, and that's just as good. But why should such a share be just as good if, as we are currently supposing, it is possessing control, and not sharing equally in something that possesses control, that makes all the difference?

It will not work, then, to establish that government power is nonarbitrary by appealing to democratic control. But I believe that better success is in the offing if we appeal instead to *accountability*. A democratic government can be accountable to its people even if the people do not control it, and accountability can be individualized to citizens in a way that control cannot. Accountability of government power to each citizen by way of democratic processes is not utopian, and it exists to a considerable (if imperfect) degree in many actual states.

Let's start by expanding on the idea of accountability, which we first encountered earlier in the context of the distinction between rights invasion and rights vitiation. In particular, let's start by returning to the professor–student relationship we considered earlier in relation to the concept of rights vitiation. A professor, we often say, is accountable to her students. The most obvious feature of this relationship is that the professor has a moral obligation to provide her students with decent instruction, fair grading, openness to their ideas as appropriate, and so forth. But this is not all that makes the professor–student relationship an accountability relationship. For the professor to be accountable to her students, a combination of additional moral and institutional components must be in place. First, the professor must owe a decent course *to her students*. That is, it must be the case not just that the professor will be guilty of wrongdoing if she fails to provide a decent course but also that any such failure will invade rights that her students hold against her. Second, and closely relatedly, the students must have standing to insist, in their own voices and on their own account, on receiving from the professor what the professor owes to them. Third, the students' standing to insist on their rights must have institutional backup. To the extent that a professor is accountable to her students, the students must be able to count on the institutional framework of the university to hear their claims, judge them on their merits, and back them up when appropriate.

It thus seems that accountability, at least insofar as it pertains to rights, has three necessary and jointly sufficient conditions. An agent, A, is accountable to another agent or group, B, to the extent that (1) A owes something to B; (2) B has standing to insist to A that A discharge her obligation; and (3) B can rely on institutional backup in support of her claim against A. Two important features of accountability so understood help distinguish it clearly from control. First, I don't need to be able to determine what another person does for her to be accountable to me. The students in our example cannot control their professor, either individually or collectively. Nevertheless, the professor is accountable to them. Second, it makes sense to say that the professor is accountable to each member of the class insofar as she is accountable to the whole class. Even if all of what the professor owes is owed to the whole class rather than to any member in isolation, each student nonetheless has good grounds to judge that her professor is accountable to her, especially if her access to mechanisms for holding professors accountable is just as good as the other students'. Accountability can individualize to the members of a group in a way that control simply cannot.

By now, you probably see the move I mean to make; government power can be nonarbitrary to the extent that it is democratically accountable to the people subject to it. But does the role of agencies in modern democracy again threaten to derail the argument? After all, modern democracies almost never have mechanisms through which citizens can directly prosecute their grievances with agencies. Arguably, this is a good reason for democracies to decrease their reliance on agencies, which is becoming ever more pronounced. Nevertheless, the distance, as it were, between the democratic public and agencies is mediated by elected officials. Agencies are accountable to elected officials for their activities, staffing, and decisions. And although democratic citizens do not control their representatives, their representatives are accountable to the democratic citizenry, so long as elections are regular, open, free, and fair. Under such democratic circumstances, government power as wielded by appointed officials and agency employees as well as by elected officials is ultimately accountable to the democratic public. For this reason, government may remedy the arbitrary power within rights endemic to the executive defect, the legislative defect, and the judicial defect without wielding arbitrary power of its own.

Two reasonable objections are likely to arise at this point. First, can we really say that ultimate accountability is just as good as direct accountability insofar as nondomination is concerned? That is, would people really be no freer within their rights if government were directly accountable to them rather than merely ultimately accountable? Second, my argument from ultimate accountability turns on the assumption that elections are regular, free, open, and fair. However, in many modern democracies, notably including the United States, elections are not nearly as free, open, or fair as one might hope, even if they are regular. I will address both concerns in the last section, which will be concerned with the limits of democratic authority. But as a foretaste, I can say this: Political legitimacy is not an all-or-nothing affair, and many modern democracies' legitimacy is fairly patchy. Nonetheless, I will argue that our political obligations typically survive such patchiness, especially where there is reasonable hope of improvement.

My argument for legitimacy, we have now seen, proceeds in two steps. The first step establishes that the state of nature's three characteristic defects prevent people from enjoying their rights. The second step establishes how the state can correct these defects without becoming an arbitrary power in its own right. This step does not appeal to the idea that majority decisions are necessarily authoritative, and it does not insist that actual laws express the majority's will. Instead, it appeals to the equal ultimate accountability of government to the people via the democratic process. In sum, democratic government is legitimate because it is necessary for people to enjoy their rights in the first place. Even if you still have reservations, just suppose for a moment that governments of at least some democratic varieties can achieve legitimacy by securing equal basic accountability to all citizens. Granting this much, we face a further problem: Why think that *only* governments can achieve legitimacy by securing equal basic accountability? Why couldn't a complex, market-driven system of private courts and security firms of the kind often imagined by anarcho-capitalists do the job just as well? If a system of anarcho-capitalist institutions could be legitimate, then government, which blocks the development of anarcho-capitalism, starts to look like an illegitimate monopoly.

I believe that government is uniquely capable of securing the equal basic accountability required for legitimacy. More specifically, any nongovernment institution or system of institutions would have to become indistinguishable from a government to attain legitimacy. To see why, it will be useful to begin with some examples from Huemer's own important treatment of what life could be like under anarcho-capitalism.

Although Huemer does not talk in terms of state of nature defects, he offers (in his earlier book on political authority) anarchistic solutions to what I have termed the legislative, executive, and judicial defects.[39] All of these solutions turn on the idea that private firms would emerge in the absence of government to offer legislative, executive, and judicial services. Like all private firms, enjoyment of their services would be contingent upon people's willingness and ability to pay their fees. Relying on basic economic principles such a standard price theory, Huemer argues that there is good reason to believe that private firms could offer legislative, executive, and judicial services more efficiently than governments offer them (or, indeed, ever could offer them). To fill out this anarcho-capitalist picture of government services more fully, it will be useful to consider in slightly more detail how Huemer imagines the firms that would offer them and those firms' relationships to their customers.

Private executive services in the form of "security firms" are a mainstay of anarcho-capitalist imagination, and they constitute the cornerstone of the market in government services that Huemer outlines. The basic idea is that individuals and corporations (e.g., commercial firms, apartment complexes, and HOAs) would be willing to pay to reduce the risk to their persons and properties

---

39. Huemer 2013, Part II.

posed by prospective rights invaders. Firms would emerge to meet this demand, and each one would offer some combination of armed protection against prospective violations and post-facto punishment in the form of militias that would hunt down and capture perpetrators. Like most services on the open market, security services would be offered at all price points at which a service provider could turn a profit, and the quality of protection available to customers would vary accordingly. To use Huemer's example, the private security on offer under anarcho-capitalism would include bare-bones "Walmart" offerings for the poor as well as luxe "Bloomingdale's" products for the rich.[40] This would, of course, mean that the wealthy "would no doubt receive higher-quality protection" than would the poor.[41] But Huemer denies that this would be a problem: "Given a fixed quantity of crime . . . I do not believe that it matters, ethically, how the crime is distributed across economic classes."[42]

In many cases, people apprehended by a private security service would deny that they did anything wrong. In those cases, it would be necessary for there to be a third party to hear appeals and render judgment. Moreover, many individuals and groups in anarcho-capitalist society would, quite apart from run-ins with security forces, encounter conflicts and disagreements for which a resolution would benefit all parties involved. To fill this role – and so to resolve what I have called the judicial defect – Huemer proposes private arbitration firms. If two subscribers to the same security service were to find themselves in need of arbitration, that firm would perhaps be able to direct them to an arbitrator with whom it holds a contract. Customers of distinct security firms could either allow their firms to choose an arbitrator for them or negotiate this point with one another directly. In any event, private arbitrators would answer the demand for conflict resolution by hearing cases and issuing verdicts. It would be irrational for a disappointed litigant to disobey an arbitrator's verdict because this would harm her reputation for trustworthiness, thereby making it harder for her to do business with others.

---

40. Huemer 2013, p. 244.
41. Huemer 2013, p. 244.
42. Huemer 2013, p. 244.

But wait: Wouldn't there need to be some standing rules for arbitrators to enforce? That is, isn't there a need for a solution to the legislative defect no less than for the executive and judicial defects? Huemer grants that there is, arguing that law could be created by a combination of precedent from prior arbitration decisions (much as "judge-made" law results from judicial precedent in common-law countries like Great Britain and the United States) and regulations created by the various organizations that individuals choose to join (e.g., HOAs).[43] Organizations could specify in their contracts the source of law to be used in arbitrations resulting from events that took place on their property.[44]

Huemer argues that a matrix of private firms of the sort just described would deliver their services more reliably and efficiently than any state could. I'm not convinced by this, but I'm happy to grant as much for the sake of argument. The really serious problem with anarcho-capitalism turns not on reliability or efficiency but rather on normative failings of anarcho-capitalism as such. In particular, anarcho-capitalist institutions fail to subject individual and group power to equal ultimate accountability. The result is rampant arbitrary power and, consequently, rights violation by vitiation. It is therefore conceptually impossible for people to live together as free and equal rights-holders under anarcho-capitalism.

To see that this so, let's consider in turn how anarcho-capitalism would address the executive, judicial, and legislative defects. Anarcho-capitalist executive agencies – that is, security firms – would be accountable only to those willing and able to buy their services. As Huemer readily admits, this would result in poorer people being entitled to claim much less good and less extensive security for their self-government, property, and other rights. Consequently, poorer people would be highly subject to others' arbitrary interference. Indeed, relatively poor people would be subject to a class of wealthy overlords with unilateral power to invade their rights at will, complete with the backing of superior security agencies to help them do so.

Similar remarks apply to arbitration firms and private courts. Whether any particular arbitration firm is accountable to an

43. Huemer 2013, pp. 271–272.
44. Huemer 2013, p. 271.

individual for rendering judgments of any particular quality – or indeed at all – turns on that individual's relative economic strength. If arbitration firm/customer pair A is economically more powerful than arbitration firm/customer pair B, A's preferences and interests will likely structure the proceedings to A's advantage and B's detriment. Similarly, if parties to a dispute must bargain, either themselves or through their security or arbitration firms, over the law that will apply with respect to a particular dispute, it stands to reason that whichever party holds greater economic leverage, and so a greater ability to hold out, will win the day and secure the choice of law that suits her best. In short, equal accountability of power with respect to rights is impossible under anarcho-capitalism, which, in turn, means that anarcho-capitalism necessarily violates rights on a massive scale. Thus, anarcho-capitalism will not do as a substitute for government.

6 Content Independence and Particularity

As I accepted at the outset of the chapter, an account of political authority must establish both content independence – the authority of government to wield power over a fairly wide and open-ended range of actions and decisions – and particularity – the authority to wield power over all and only its citizens (and relevant visitors – more on them later) in particular. This means that it is necessary to establish content independence and particularity for each of the two dimensions of political authority, namely political legitimacy and political obligation. Consequently, our final task before turning to obligation in the next section is to state explicitly how the account of legitimacy on offer here establishes content independence and particularity.

Let's take content independence first. On the face of it, it might seem that legitimacy as I have endorsed it ranges only over a very narrow range of actions and choices. For on my account, government legitimacy depends on government's resolving the three defects that make it impossible for people to enjoy freedom within self-government and property outside of the state. Consequently, government power is legitimate only to the extent that it secures its citizens' freedom within self-government and property. This might seem to entail that governments can only be legitimate to the extent that they restrict their activities to preventing people from interfering with one another's bodies, actions, and property. Real states in the modern world, however, do enormously more than this, from funding research and the arts to operating all manner of welfare programs. Thus, it might seem that even if I am right about the relationship between government and rights, this does not secure content independence of the sort necessary to show that modern democracies – or indeed any states very much like them – are legitimate.

Since my account does, indeed, turn on governments' securing freedom within rights, legitimate government power cannot extend beyond the power necessary for citizens to enjoy their rights without subjection to arbitrary power. Thus, the account is not totally content independent. Admitting this much is hardly a problem, however, because as Huemer rightly notes, no theory of legitimacy could reasonably hold that there are literally no limits to the content of legitimate government power. Nevertheless, it is important to show that legitimacy is content independent at least to an extent that will allow government power to extend roughly as far as it extends in the best-functioning contemporary democracies. Happily, I believe that such content independence is well within reach. This is because (a) self-government and property need very considerable expansion and elaboration to facilitate decent social and economic life under anything like realistic circumstances and (b) there is permanent, reasonable disagreement about both the extent and the content of that expansion and elaboration.

Let's begin with the need for expansion and elaboration of basic rights within a complex society. We encountered this need once already in our discussion of the legislative defect. People cannot author and pursue complex lives within a diverse array of civil and economic institutions if they have rights only to their own bodies and to physical objects directly connected with their bodily action. Just think of the myriad claims people need to hold against one another to live anything like full lives in modern society; from health care to finance, from education to church, people need reliable ranges of choice within which others are accountable not to interfere. For these rights to be adequately definite, enforceable, and justiciable, government must define, enforce, and adjudicate them. Thus, rightful freedom allows, and indeed requires, legitimate government action to range over a wide range of actions and choices.

It is important to point out that the range of legitimate government power just described is not just wide, but (largely) open-ended. Although self-government and property require substantial expansion and elaboration for people securely to the author and execute their own plans as independent equals, these basic rights do not, in and of themselves, call for any particular pattern of expansion and elaboration. We can see this simply by observing that different societies expand and elaborate basic rights in different ways to serve the same purposes and that they do so with comparable success. For instance, a functioning modern society must include structures of rights that allow people to sue one another. If people did not share equally in some such structure of rights, they would not have the standing to hold one another to account for observing the norms that make it possible for them to live together as independent equals. But this does not entail that any particular system of tort law is uniquely correct, right down to its finest details. To the contrary, there is a (limited) range of reasonable ways to distribute risk and responsibility within tort law, and there is reasonable disagreement both between different communities and within particular communities about how best to do so. The legitimacy of democratic government's power is content independent insofar as that power legitimately selects from within this range and enforces its selection in the community it governs.

This last observation brings us to our second main point about content independence: all modern democratic states contain permanent reasonable disagreement on most morally significant matters. Following Kevin Vallier, we may call this state of affairs "evaluative pluralism."[45] People subscribe to a wide range of incompatible worldviews and value systems, and, as equal self-governors, they have a right to do so and to live accordingly, at least to the extent compatible with everyone else doing the same. Deep disagreement within political communities extends not just to how government should expand and elaborate basic rights but also to which parts of life are open to government action. We reasonably disagree not just about how the government should carry out the work that properly falls to it but also on what that work is and how far into our lives it extends.

To bear out these two dimensions of reasonable disagreement about state action, it will be useful to consider a contemporary example: pharmaceutical testing and approval. In most

---

45. Vallier 2018, p. 20.

contemporary democracies, including the United States, the government uses an agency (the FDA in the United States) to control which drugs may legally be prescribed, sold, and consumed and to establish a regime of testing on which approval depends. In the United States, there is a wide range of disagreement about how stringent the FDA's testing and certification procedure should be, with some people arguing for a speedier process and others arguing for a more cautious one. Most members of the two major American political parties, however, agree that government power properly extends to pharmaceutical regulation, including prohibiting the sale of drugs that fail to meet testing standards. But some libertarians argue that there is no proper procedure through which the FDA should control access to drugs because the state has no standing to control that access in the first place, even if it does have standing to offer safety information to individuals considering whether or not to take a particular drug.[46] There is thus disagreement both about *how* the government should govern access to pharmaceuticals and about *whether* it should do so.

All of the positions in this debate are facially reasonable, and all of them turn on the question of how to interpret self-government and property. Those who accept that the government ought to license drugs reason that since we must be able to rely on safe and effective medicine in order to plan our lives – or, indeed, to even *live* our lives – as independent equals, the state has standing to legislate, execute, and judge with respect to the quality and safety of drugs and keep those that fail off the market. Within this broad camp, people disagree about how government can best support rightful freedom in this domain. Those who endorse a more aggressive FDA hold that the risk of harmful drugs – and, perhaps especially, of private firms rushing products to market against the public interest – justifies very strict gatekeeping. By contrast, those who endorse a more lenient FDA hold that self-government tilts toward more space for individuals (and, perhaps, drug companies) to assess risks and work out mutually acceptable terms without government oversight. Finally, those who hold that the government should play no role at all in licensing drugs and regulating their consumption argue that if we are self-governors, we should enjoy

---

46. Flanigan 2017, Chapter 2.

absolute noninterference in all matters pertaining directly to our bodies, drugs very much included. These positions on the relationship between self-government and government agencies like the FDA are all reasonable and defensible. Nevertheless, only one of them can apply to a particular political community at a particular time. Democratically accountable government may settle the matter and legitimately enforce its verdict. For if it did not, we would simply be subject to the arbitrary power of the strongest ideological faction (or else to the sort of anarcho-capitalism we rejected in the last section).

The example of disagreement about the FDA brings out a more general point: Questions of both the proper sphere of government power and how government ought to use its power within that sphere are subject to disagreement that is fundamental, intractable, and reasonable. This means that there is a very wide range of content that government law and policy can have while remaining within the scope of reasonable disagreement about how to legislate, enforce, and adjudicate our basic rights. Consequently, government action, subject to ultimate democratic accountability, is legitimate anywhere within this range. For whenever it acts within this range, it plays its legitimate role of correcting the defects that make it impossible for us to enjoy rightful freedom as independent equals outside of the state.

So much for content independence. What, though, of particularity? As we have now observed many times over, government power is legitimate only to the extent that it rectifies the three defects that frustrate rightful freedom among equals in nonpolitical circumstances. Thus, the power of a government is legitimate over all of the people for whom it performs this service. Such people may be divided into three classes.

First, and most obviously, legitimate power extends to all resident citizens and other permanent residents. For all of these people depend on the state for the possibility of conducting their lives as independent equals who are free within their rights.

Second, legitimate power extends to expatriate citizens who, though not currently living in their home country, continue to have their rights and relationships protected and structured by their home government. I, for instance, am in England as I type these words, but much of my life – my entire financial and vocational life, as well as much of my real and personal property – continue to be defined and secured by rights stated and guaranteed under U.S. law. The

U.S. government continues to secure many of my rights and rightful relationships, and to the extent that it does so, its power over me – to levy taxes on me, for instance – is legitimate.

Third, and finally, legitimate government power extends to include voluntary temporary visitors insofar as they make use of the protections of the government they are visiting. Indeed, such visitors are the only people who plausibly count as genuine tacit consenters to political power. As Locke puts the point, those who decide to visit a foreign government for a time are legitimately subject to its laws in much the way that a person might be subject to the dictates of a person "in whose family he found it convenient to abide for some time."[47] Thus, insofar as I am living in England for the time being, the government of the United Kingdom may legitimately impose its relevant laws on me.

Now let's consider why a government's power would not be legitimate if that government attempted to exercise it over people who fall into none of these categories – why, for instance, the government of the United States may not enforce its decisions on Germans living in Germany or on Nigerians living in Nigeria (or, for that matter, in Germany). Little needs to be said on this front; if a government does not secure rightful freedom for someone in any respect, then it, of course, has no legitimate power over her. After all, legitimate government power is nothing more or less than power that serves to correct the defects of the state of nature with respect to some community of people, thereby making it possible for them to enjoy their rights as independent equals. If a government does not perform this service for someone, it does not relate to that person as a government and so has no standing to subject them to its laws.

7 Obligation

We have now seen why government power can be legitimate in a way that is both content independent and particularized. With this much in hand, we may now turn to political obligation. Even if I am right about legitimacy, why do citizens have moral obligations to obey the state?

---

47. *Second Treatise* 22.

The basic structure of my answer to this question is identical to the structure of the argument from equality that Huemer criticizes briefly in the first chapter.[48] It is different, however, with respect to its content. Whereas that argument turns on the obligation to respect others by treating their *interests* as equally important, my argument for authority turns on respecting others by treating their *rights* as equally important. I grant Huemer's criticisms of the argument from equality in its interest-based form, but I will argue that it succeeds in the altered, rights-based form that I endorse.

According to the argument from equality as Huemer presents it, citizens are obligated to obey their democratic governments because it is obligatory to respect others' equality, and respecting others' equality demands that we not treat our own desires and preferences as more important than theirs simply because they are ours. If we disobey the laws of our democratic government, which is accountable to all for treating every vote, complaint, and referendum, equally, we disrespect our fellow citizens. As Huemer puts it, if you disobey, "you are in effect treating your own judgment or desires as being of greater weight than the judgment or desires of other people."

Huemer criticizes this argument on three grounds. First, it is not the case (because of agencies, improper accountability, and so forth) that the laws of any actual democracy reflect the judgments of a majority of its citizens. So, whatever the merits of the argument in principle, it fails in practice. Second, even if the laws of actual democracies did reflect the judgments of a majority of their citizens, a group's majority decision is still answerable to the rights of each group member. Thus, if I am a member of a group of diners, the group has no moral standing to make me pay for everyone even if a majority of the group says that I should. Third, and most importantly, it is not plausible that there is a moral duty to treat people as equals in any sense other than as bearers of equal rights. Since, according to Huemer, there is no need to obey democratic laws to respect others as equal bearers of rights, we may not infer a duty to obey the law, democratic or otherwise, from a duty to respect others as equals.

---

48. The version of the argument from equality that Huemer criticizes is a simplified version of Thomas Christiano's (2008) argument for state authority.

As I have already discussed, I agree with Huemer that we may not assume that particular laws are subject to majority control and that we consequently may not assume that they express majority decisions. But I have also already argued that it is not majority control that makes democracy respect equality but rather equal ultimate accountability. Thus, the first objection is not a problem for my account. The same goes for the second objection: I don't assign any moral power to majority decisions simply as such, and I do not believe that such decisions can override anyone's rights. As for the third objection, I agree completely: It is not plausible that we are obligated to respect others as equals in any sense other than as equal bearers of rights. However, we have seen that it is exactly this kind of equality – equality within rights – that democratic government uniquely makes possible. It is only under democratic government that it is possible for people to enjoy their rights because it is only under democratic government that the expansion, enforcement, and adjudication of rights are not subject to arbitrary power. We need democratic governments to live as equal rights holders, so the duty to respect one another's equality requires us to respect democratic law.

Let's try to spell out this thought in greater detail, step-by-step. First, the function of rights is to secure rights-holders within a particular domain of choice or action. So, for instance, to enjoy the right of free speech, it is not enough that no one invades it – that is, that no one forces me, or tries to force me, to alter my speech. Additionally, whether I get to exercise my right must not depend on anyone else's will, say-so, or sheer power. If I get to speak as I see fit only to the extent that someone else feels like letting me, I do not enjoy my right to speak my mind – I am not free within it – even if those in power over me *do* decide to let me exercise it. Thus, for some plurality of people to enjoy equal rights equally, they need to be free from one another's arbitrary power within the scope of their rights.

Second, we saw in the previous section that wherever people live together without government, their rightful relations to one another suffer from three defects, each of which subjects rights to arbitrary power: the executive defect, the legislative defect, and the judicial defect. Without a democratic state that is ultimately equally accountable to all members of the group, there is no way to enforce, extend, or interpret rights in a way that addresses adequately the problem of arbitrary power within rights. But since the whole point of rights is to secure important choices against arbitrary power, this situation is in tension with equal rights. Therefore, democratic government power is legitimate, not despite the moral authority of rights but on account of that moral authority.

Now for the third and final step, which connects the foregoing reasoning to an obligation to obey the laws of democratic governments. If I am a citizen of a properly democratic state but insist on flouting the law and doing as I see fit, I treat my own will and judgment as unaccountable to the structure of law that makes it possible for people to live together as equal rights holders. That is, I treat myself as a having arbitrary power over others. And if I treat others as subject to my arbitrary power, I do not treat them as rights holders equal to myself. In short, I fail to respect their equal rights. So, we may grant that Huemer is quite right; the only kind of equality we are obligated to respect in others is equality of rights. But to respect our fellow citizens' equality of rights, we must obey the law that is equally accountable to all of us alike.

Let's now bear out this line of reasoning still further with a real-life example. Suppose that I find myself in a position to cheat on my taxes without any significant likelihood of being caught; perhaps I received some extra cash income from odd jobs that no employer reported to the Internal Revenue Service. Further suppose that I would donate any money saved by cheating to a fund for mosquito nets in developing countries and that this use is plausibly of greater moral significance than the purposes to which the government would put my money. Regardless of the moral merit of my plans for the money I would save by falsely reporting my income, I am obligated to report my income correctly and pay the taxes levied on it. For if I ignore tax law and pursue my own purposes in violation of it, I treat my will as having arbitrary authority over the very structure of law that makes it possible for my fellow citizens and me to live together as equal rights bearers. Insofar as I have a moral duty to respect others' rights, I have a duty to subordinate my own (possibly meritorious) purposes to public purposes and, ultimately, to pay my taxes.

Before moving on to consider the limits of political authority, we should note briefly that the grounds of content independence and particularity that apply to legitimacy also apply to obligation. Political obligation is (largely – we'll discuss exceptions shortly) content independent insofar as democratically accountable law within the space of reasonable disagreement makes it possible for us to live together with our equal rights intact despite such disagreement. That is, we are obligated to obey democratically accountable law within the space of reasonable disagreement because such law corrects the state of nature's defects, not because it corrects them in any one particular way. Moreover, political obligation to governments is particularized to their citizens and relevant visitors because it is a state's citizens and relevant visitors whose rights that state secures, thereby creating the grounds on which individuals owe respect to one another through respect for the law.

8   The Limits of Political Authority

With the core of my account of political authority now complete, I take up in this final section problems that arise on the margins of democratic life, where democratic norms break down procedurally, substantively, or both. Do democratic states still have authority when they suffer from serious structural flaws or pass immoral laws? And if there are limits to democratic authority under such conditions, where are those limits, and why? Let's start with procedural failings before turning to substantively unjust laws.

Perhaps the most egregious and frequently discussed procedural failing in American political life is the role private money plays in federal, state, and local elections. In the United States, people running for office must raise money to support the various communications and publicity efforts (e.g., advertising, media spots, "door-knocking," social media, etc.) necessary to conduct a successful modern campaign for office. In most cases, individuals and corporations are limited by law to fairly modest direct donations to campaigns. However, "political action committees," or PACs, may organize, independently of any formal campaign, to raise and spend limitless money on behalf of their chosen candidates. As a result, individuals and corporations can – and do – wield enormous power over candidates' platforms and eventual voting behavior while in office. Significant federal, state, and even local campaigns turn very heavily on the interests of wealthy entities that are willing and able to pour tens of millions of dollars (or even hundreds of millions of dollars) into PAC coffers. This method of funding elections is obviously in deep tension with the idea that government should be equally basically accountable to all citizens. For it has the consequence that elected officials are disproportionately accountable to those citizens who can afford to spend large sums on PACs.[49]

Even if we put aside the pernicious role of PAC power in U.S. campaign finance, elections themselves are also beset with problems that undermine equal basic accountability. Many politicians benefit (or believe that they benefit) from low election turnouts, especially among poor people and members of racial minorities.[50] Consequently, elected assemblies, especially at the state level, have frequently erected barriers to voting that disproportionately affect the poor, members of minorities, or both. For instance, since 2016, some states have conducted voter "purges" to remove from the rolls of eligible voters anyone who has not voted for several years.[51] Moreover, many states have passed voter-ID laws with the expectation that citizens of the opposing party will be less likely to have a valid ID. To the extent that an electoral procedure is more accountable to those who are rich and white than it is to those who are poor and non-white, the government whose offices that procedure fills is not equally basically accountable to the citizenry.

If troubles with campaign finance and voting access are not enough to undermine your confidence in equal basic accountability within American democracy, consider gerrymandering. One need only look at an electoral map of state like Ohio to see congressional districts which, rather than tracing the boundaries of counties or cities, writhe across the landscape in weirdly contorted slivers. This is because parties in power are permitted to draw (equally populated) electoral districts largely as they see fit. And parties in power unfailingly use that power to "pack" and "split" the population in ways that will deliver them as many seats as possible. As North Carolina state representative David Lewis said in 2016: "I propose that we draw the maps to give a partisan advantage to 10

49. On the evils of American campaign finance and possible solutions, see Lessig 2011.
50. President Trump, for instance, recently claimed that if levels of voting get too high, his own Republican party will no longer have a realistic shot at winning elections (Blake 2020).
51. Casey 2019.

Republicans and three Democrats, because I do not believe it's possible to draw a map with 11 Republicans and two Democrats."[52] To the extent that ruling parties warp the electoral map to favor their own members, government is not equally basically accountable to all citizens.

In many instances, then, modern democracies fail to maintain democratic procedures that fully secure equal basic accountability to all citizens. This means that regardless of whether they wield their executive, judicial, and legislative functions in a way that secures rightful independence among citizens, they fail fully to avoid wielding arbitrary power of their own. Unfortunately, though, the trouble doesn't stop there. In addition to these procedural failings, modern democracies sometimes also pass, adjudicate, and enforce law that has no rightful justification and invades rights.

Some examples will drive home the reality and severity of substantive injustice within U.S. law. As I write, Americans are protesting several recent police killings of unarmed black men. They are responding to one of the most damning facts about American law: Police officers regularly harass, injure, and even kill people – disproportionately black people – and they overwhelmingly get away with it.[53] Furthermore, there is usually no point in appealing to the courts for help, as American courts rely on a doctrine of "qualified immunity" for police officers that shields police officers from a wide swath of civil liability. In short, the American state maintains armies of unaccountable soldiers who can and do exercise arbitrary power to the severe detriment of others.

Now consider one of the most egregious examples of American offshore misbehavior: the prison facility at Guantanamo Bay, Cuba. The United States is currently holding foreign nationals there without trial, access to attorneys, or release dates. Over the past several decades, the United States has tortured some of these prisoners and openly defended its purported standing to do so. Moreover, although the current spate of torture and imprisonment got underway during George W. Bush's Republican administration, Barack Obama's Democratic administration never closed the facility,

52. Hise and Lewis 2019.
53. On the disproportionate rate of black deaths at the hands of police, see DeGue et al. 2016.

despite Obama's repeated false claims that closure was imminent.[54] The U.S. government has simply decided that it is in its interests to invade horribly the basic rights of the prisoners at Guantanamo Bay, and it appears ready to continue doing so for the foreseeable future.

To the extent that the United States has, like many other nations, failed to protect rights and to secure government's equal basic accountability, it is a less fully legitimate state than it would otherwise be. Given my argument so far, I could hardly say otherwise. If states are legitimate insofar as they (a) allow people to enjoy their rights without arbitrary power among them and (b) avoid becoming arbitrary powers in their own right, then states that engage in the kind of behavior I have been describing cannot be fully legitimate.

Nevertheless, it is important to distinguish between two kinds of imperfectly legitimate states. In one class, there are what we may call **flawed states**. Such states, which include most modern democracies – the United States, Germany, Japan, etc. – for the most part secure rightful freedom within a structure of basic equal accountability even while falling short on multiple important fronts. In the cases of most such states, severe failures of substantive and procedural justice are all the more jarring because they occur against a basically democratic, rights-securing institutional backdrop. In the other class, there are **failed states**. These are states that have either a nondemocratic form of government or a radically inadequate democracy (one that bans women or members of certain racial groups from participation, say), or that broadly fail to secure and expand property and self-government on any plausible interpretation of those rights. Cuba, with its autocratic one-party rule and substantial ban on private economic activity, is an example of a failed state. Other examples include (monarchist, sexist) Saudi Arabia and (communist, absolutist) Venezuela.[55]

Do denizens of flawed states and failed states have a duty to obey them? The answer with respect to failed states is easy: no. Since failed states are totally illegitimate, no one has any duty to obey

---

54. Bruck 2016.
55. Stilz draws a similar distinction between two classes of states that fail to be fully substantively and procedurally adequate, albeit without the terminology I introduce here (Stilz 2009, pp. 85–85).

them. There may, of course, be other reasons for the subjects of such states to obey them. Perhaps most obviously, it will usually be prudent to obey, as disobedience might result in violence, imprisonment, or both. Moreover, a failed state might provide services that cannot be easily replicated under the (oppressive, unjust) circumstances, and disrupting those services might be wrong despite the illegitimacy of the power overseeing them. What we may safely conclude, though, is that denizens of failed states never have moral reasons to obey that are grounded in a right to rule held by those in power.[56]

The moral situation with respect to flawed states, however, is quite different. Except for special circumstances that call for civil disobedience (which we will consider shortly), citizens of flawed states have a duty to obey the law. This is because, as we have already discussed, each of us has a more basic duty to respect one another's rights by respecting the institutions that accountably define and secure them, and flawed states accountably define and secure their citizens' rights more effectively than any available institution other than improved versions of those same states. Put another way, citizens of a flawed state face a choice: either use their current state as the institutional framework that their rights demand while trying to improve it or disband and try to build something new from scratch. As long as a state remains merely flawed rather than failed, the first choice – stick with it and work to improve it – better respects citizens' rights than simply reverting to the state of nature and trying again. Consequently, individual citizens should respect their flawed states' laws to respect one another as equal rights-holders.

To bear out this conception of political obligation to flawed states, it will be useful to return to the American context. Inegalitarian campaign finance and myriad electoral inequities together make the U.S. government far from equally basically accountable to each member of the electorate. However, it is nonetheless true that American elections, as well as American processes for raising referendums, engaging in public comment, and protesting government decisions, are substantially free and fair. Consequently, one of the most important questions that citizens must address is how

---

56. Simmons 1979 is the classic source for the view that people may have reasons to obey the state even if it lacks a right to rule.

best to improve governmental procedure so that they can relate to one another as fully independent within their rights. But since their shared government is sufficiently procedurally adequate to establish and secure equality within rights to a significant degree – a degree much greater than would be possible without democratic government – our duty to respect others' rights by obeying the law survives, barring special circumstances that call for civil disobedience. We must respect others by respecting the legal apparatus that makes our freedom as rights bearers possible even if that legal apparatus is seriously in need of repair.

Under flawed conditions like our own, however, obedience is not sufficient to respect our fellow citizens. Additionally, each citizen is obligated to work actively to improve the procedures that damage equal basic accountability. At a bare minimum, this means that all citizens must vote, and vote well – that is, after careful research on the issues and deliberation with others.[57] But this is likely not enough. Given how fundamental government is to our freedom within our rights, we usually have a duty to take part more actively in reforming our political community. Exactly how, and to what extent, each person should do this is a question for another day. My point here is simply this: to respect each other as bearers of equal rights, citizens of flawed states must, barring civil disobedience, both obey the laws and work actively for change. Insofar as government constitutes the framework through which we respect one another as equals, we owe it to one another to take part in the work of making that framework adequate to its moral role.

Aside: Does My Vote Matter?

It is very unlikely that any one vote will make the difference in an election. Does this mean that it is irrational to vote? In her recent book, Julia Maskivker argues that those who conclude that voting is irrational on the grounds that one's vote is unlikely to be decisive apply a mistaken standard of what it takes for participation in a collective effort to be rational. Most people tend to agree that it is not only rational but

---

57. Maskivker 2019.

also morally required to refrain from taking part in a harmful group action, even if any one person's participation is unlikely to make any difference to the outcome. For instance, it is not only rational but also morally required to refrain from taking part in a group stoning of a purported religious heretic even if it will make no difference to the outcome whether you throw any stones. Similarly, it might be rational – and even morally required – to actively take part in a collective action (such as voting for decent leaders or policies) to whose outcome your individual contribution is almost certain not to be decisive.

Although citizens are generally obligated to obey the laws of their flawed states, disobedience can nonetheless be warranted; sometimes, laws are simply too immoral to command our obedience. In those cases, it is usually obligatory to disobey publicly and in full view of our fellow citizens and to accept legal prosecution for our disobedience. In the rest of this section, I'll first consider how citizens ought to disobey under conditions that merit disobedience before attempting to identify those conditions.

Let's begin with an important but often overlooked distinction between two ways in which citizens might violate laws they judge to be immoral.[58] First, there is **conscientious refusal**. This is simply a citizen's noncompliance with a law on moral grounds. It may take place in private or even in secret, and it does not include or entail any element of communication, let alone an attempt to alter law or a cry for justice to fellow citizens. For example, if a committed anarchist secretly cheats on her taxes because she judges that taxation is immoral, this is a case of conscientious refusal. Second, there is **civil disobedience**, for which we may simply borrow Huemer's helpful definition: "Civil disobedience is a practice wherein individuals openly disobey the law or other government commands due to moral objections to the law, usually with the hope of prompting social change." A citizen engages in civil disobedience when she violates an immoral law in a way that is public and intended to

---

58. The distinction between conscientious refusal and civil disobedience follows Rawls 1999, pp. 319–326 and, more recently, Klosko 2019, pp. 109–119.

communicate her judgment to her fellow citizens with the ultimate aim of changing the law. Thus, as Rawls puts the point, civil disobedience "expresses disobedience to law within the limits of fidelity to law, although it is at the outer edge thereof."[59]

Insofar as it is permissible for citizens of flawed states to break the law at all, it is usually mandatory for them to engage in civil disobedience rather than mere conscientious refusal.[60] This is because insofar as there is a moral reason for a citizen of such a state to disobey, there is a reason for her to do so in a way that affirms and respects each of her fellow citizens as such. Two features of civil disobedience play an especially important role in preserving this kind of civic respect for others in the face of disobedience.

First, civilly disobedient citizens can and should communicate to other citizens not just that a particular law is unjust and should be changed, but also why it is unjust and should be changed. This is because, on the assumption that the state is merely flawed rather than failed, disobedience takes place against a moral background that requires that one not arrogate the legislative, executive, or judicial functions of the state to oneself. Thus, to the extent that I am justified in disobeying in a particular case, I have a duty to subject this disobedience to the judgment of my fellow citizens, to whom government – and so the law – is ultimately basically accountable. And to subject my disobedience to my fellow citizens' judgment, I must communicate to them where and why injustice is so intolerable as to merit disobedience. Black Lives Matter protestors lying down to block a freeway is a good example. By blocking the road in a way that mimics the dead bodies of black Americans murdered by the police, they say: People are being murdered, and the ordinary flow of life – and traffic – simply cannot go on until the law and practice surrounding police accountability are fundamentally changed.

Second, civilly disobedient citizens should not try to evade criminal or civil legal proceedings that result from their disobedience. Huemer disagrees:

> If the state has legitimate authority, then how could the disobedience be justified to begin with? One might say that the state

59. Rawls 1999, p. 322.
60. Cf. Brownlee 2012.

has legitimate authority *in general*, but that certain *particular* laws are illegitimate. But in that case, wouldn't the *punishment* under those *particular* laws also be illegitimate?[61]

The right answer is that civilly disobedient citizens should submit to legal proceedings for reasons much like those that require civilly disobedient citizens to communicate clearly to their fellow citizens why they think disobedience is called for. Insofar as my fellow citizens and I share a legal framework that constitutes our equal freedom within our rights, my duty to respect them as equal rights-holders requires me to submit my decision to disobey to the community's more basic legal norms and procedures. In particular, civilly disobedient citizens should not attempt to evade either court proceedings or any penalties those proceedings might render. To do otherwise would be to treat one's own will and judgment as sovereign over others, and that would disrespect them and their equal rights. A civilly disobedient citizen who accepts the legal consequences of her disobedience thereby accepts the equality of her status under law even while making an especially desperate and liminal plea to her fellow citizens.[62]

So much for how citizens ought to disobey when civil disobedience is called for. But when *is* it called for? The correct answer, I believe, is as simple as it is frustrating: Each citizen must decide for herself, in consultation with others and the moral resources at her disposal, whether she faces a law so iniquitous that it fails to meet the threshold of reasonable disagreement. Moreover, the moral stakes of a decision to disobey are quite high; decide wrongly, and you disrespect your fellow citizens as equal rights-holders. But although we all must face these moral stakes without direction from the state, it would be quite mistaken to suggest that decisions about whether to engage in civil disobedience must – or even may – amount to merely doing as we please. Once again, Rawls is helpful on this point:

---

61. Huemer, this book, Chapter 1, Section 6, p. 59.
62. Rawls 1999, p. 322. For a contrary position, see Brownlee 2012.

While each person must decide for himself whether the circumstances justify civil disobedience, it does not follow that one is to decide as one pleases. It is not by looking to our personal interests, or to our political allegiances narrowly construed, that we should make up our minds. To act autonomously and responsibly a citizen must look to the political principles that underlie and guide the interpretation of the constitution. He must try to assess how these principles should be applied in the existing circumstances. If he comes to the conclusion after due consideration that civil disobedience is justified and conducts himself accordingly, he acts conscientiously. And though he may be mistaken, he has not done as he pleased.[63]

It will be useful to conclude this section by considering some concrete scenarios that raise the question of civil disobedience. Each one is meant to reflect a difficult decision about obedience that a citizen of a flawed democracy might encounter in her everyday life. Let's start with an old standard: drugs. In the United States and many other countries, possessing, using, or transferring most mind-altering drugs (other than alcohol, which enjoys unique cultural prestige) is illegal and, in many cases, subject to harsh criminal sanctions. Many citizens (your author included) judge that these laws violate self-government and are consequently unjust. Others, however, deny that they violate any right. As they see the matter, self-government doesn't extend to using, possessing, or transferring drugs any more than it extends to punching other people in the nose. After all, most would agree that drugs can be seriously harmful in a variety of ways, and drug-related acts by individuals almost always take place within a context of markets and cultural practices that facilitate widespread drug use and, consequently, dependence. Since those markets and cultural practices harm others, including nonconsenting others (think of the families of users or of those who have become chemically addicted), anti-drug laws are required by respect for equal rights under law. For several reasons – some of them articulated by John Stuart Mill

---

63. Rawls 1999, p. 341.

long ago – I don't believe that this argument succeeds.[64] However, it is hardly unreasonable on its face. Thus, when adequately democratic governments pass laws banning recreational drugs, citizens ought to obey them.

Now consider another issue never far from the public mind: taxes. There are many flawed democracies in which taxes on personal income are quite high. In Denmark, for instance, the maximum effective income tax rate on income over approximately $85,000 is over 50%.[65] If our capacity to develop and pursue self-authored economic goals in the market (e.g., investing capital or developing a business) is a fundamental liberty closely connected to self-government, then it is plausible that this rate of taxation is unjust.[66] Others, however, argue that it is only against the kind of institutional background of social services and guarantees that such taxes fund that meaningful self-government is even possible. Although both positions cannot be right, both clearly fall within the domain of reasonable disagreement. Thus, those Danes who hold, perhaps even very strongly and for well-considered reasons, that such high taxes are unjust are nonetheless obligated to pay up.

In the past two cases, I rendered the judgment that disobedience is unwarranted. But as we discussed earlier, this is not always so. As I write, the United States is suffering under a regime of immigration law, mostly enforced by an agency called Immigration and Customs Enforcement (or ICE), that sanctions such brutal practices as separating undocumented families and caging their members, including the children.[67] This is, in my judgment and that of many others, a fundamental rights invasion that no one could reasonably endorse. Consequently, citizens should not cooperate with ICE raids on undocumented communities even if this means directly disobeying orders from law enforcement. However, as I argued earlier, this moral license to disobey comes at a price; in order to afford our fellow citizens the kind of respect that we usually manifest by obeying the law, we must

---

64. Mill famously argues that the close connection between human flourishing and individual discretion to engage in risky behavior should lead us to be very reluctant to sanction such behavior unless it harms someone else "directly, and in the first instance" (Mill 1989, p. 15).
65. Wiking 2016.
66. Tomasi 2012.
67. Cheatham 2020.

not hide our disobedience. Instead, our disobedience should be public and communicative. We must make it known not only that we have disobeyed but also why we believe we were justified in doing so and why the relevant laws should be changed. If this leads to criminal charges or civil litigation, we must go to court, defend our position, and accept the results. If I were to try to evade the legal process after (rightly) defying ICE, this would amount to treating the United States not just as a flawed state with some – indeed, many – bad laws but as a failed state. For reasons we have now discussed at length, this would disrespect my fellow citizens and their equal rights.

Someone might object that not everyone would agree with me about whether these cases fall within the range of reasonable disagreement about how best to respect equal rights under law. This is, of course, quite true. But there is no avoiding this problem; ultimately, each citizen bears the responsibility of judging for herself when respect for others' rights calls for civil disobedience. All we can do is recognize how serious a matter civil disobedience is, think things through as well as we can, and then commit ourselves to the course that what we can no longer in good conscience avoid.

Finally, let's return to a matter that Huemer considers at some length: jury nullification. Although I have largely been disagreeing with his arguments in this section so far, here we agree, albeit not, perhaps, for quite the same reasons. Huemer writes: "The jury's job is *not* just to evaluate the factual evidence; the jury's job is to serve as the conscience of the community and as a check on government power." I couldn't agree more. Regardless of the negative remarks about jury nullification that certain judges may choose to include in jury instructions, juries' power to nullify is clearly built into the legal structure of the United States and many other nations through the conjunction of juries' power to render verdicts and the prohibition of double jeopardy. Jury nullification, like civil disobedience, is an opportunity for citizens to reject particular laws while respecting – indeed, in order to respect – the law as a whole. It is an avenue for citizens to reject *a* law in order affirm *the* law by holding government power accountable to the moral judgments of the community.

9 Conclusion

Each of us has a natural duty to respect one another as equal rights holders. This means that each of us has a duty to conduct ourselves in ways that not only avoid invading others' rights but also respect the conditions necessary for people to live together without the arbitrary power that vitiates rights. Democratic government subject to equal basic accountability to the citizenry uniquely institutes those conditions by rectifying the three state of nature defects – the executive defect, the judicial defect, and the legislative defect – that make it impossible for people sharing a physical environment to enjoy their rights. Only democratic government can rectify these defects because only democratic government can be equally basically accountable to everyone subject to it. Although there are limits to political authority, and although civil disobedience is sometimes called for, adequately democratic states largely have a right to rule, and their citizens normally have an obligation to obey their laws.

References

Applbaum, Arthur Isak. 2019. *Legitimacy: The Right to Rule in a Wanton World*. Cambridge, MA: Harvard University Press.

Blake, Aaron. 2020, March 30. "Trump Just Comes Out and Says It: The GOP Is Hurt When It's Easier to Vote", *The Washington Post* (online).

Brownlee, Kimberlee. 2012. *Conscience and Conviction: The Case for Civil Disobedience*. Oxford: Oxford University Press.

Bruck, Connie. 2016, August 1. "Why Obama Has Failed to Close Guantánamo", *The New Yorker* (online).

Casey, Nicholas. 2019, October 30. "Georgia Plans to Purge 300,000 Names From Its Voter Rolls", *The New York Times* (online).

Cheatham, Amelia. 2020, February 10. "U.S. Detention of Child Migrants", *U.S. Council on Foreign Relations* (online).

Christiano, Thomas. 2008. *The Constitution of Equality: Democratic Authority and Its Limits*. New York: Oxford University Press.

Christmas, Billy. 2021. "Against Kantian Statism", *Journal of Politics* (forthcoming).

Darwall, Stephen. 2006. *The Second Person Standpoint: Morality, Respect, and Accountability*. Cambridge, MA: Harvard University Press.

DeGue et al. 2016. "Deaths Due to Use of Lethal Force by Law Enforcement Findings From the National Violent Death Reporting System, 17 U.S. States, 2009–2012", *American Journal of Preventative Medicine* 51 (5; supplement 3): 173–187.

Feinberg, Joel. 1970. "The Nature and Value of Rights", *Journal of Value Inquiry* 4 (4): 243–260.

Flanigan, Jessica. 2017. *Pharmaceutical Freedom: Why Patients Have a Right to Self-Medicate*. New York: Oxford University Press.

Hart, H.L.A. 1982. *Essays on Bentham: Studies in Jurisprudence and Political Theory*. Oxford: Clarendon Press.

Hise, Ralph and David Lewis. 2019, March 25. "We Drew Congressional Maps for Partisan Advantage. That Was the Point", *The Atlantic* (online).

Hohfeld, Wesley Newcomb. 1923. *Fundamental Legal Conceptions as Applied in Judicial Reasoning and Other Essays*. New Haven: Yale University Press.

Huemer, Michael. 2013. *The Problem of Political Authority: An Examination of the Right to Coerce and the Duty to Obey*. New York: Palgrave MacMillan.

Kant, Immanuel. 1996. *The Metaphysics of Morals*, ed. and trans. Mary Gregor. Cambridge: Cambridge University Press.

Klosko, George. 2019. *Why Should We Obey the Law?* Medford, MA: Polity.

Lessig, Laurence. 2011. *Republic, Lost: How Money Corrupts Congress – And a Plan to Stop It*. New York: Grand Central Publishing.

List, Christian and Philip Pettit. 2011. *Group Agency: The Possibility, Design, and Status of Corporate Agents*. New York: Oxford University Press.

Locke, John. 1988. *Two Treatises of Government*, ed. Peter Laslett. Cambridge: Cambridge University Press.

Maskivker, Julia. 2019. *The Duty to Vote*. New York: Oxford University Press.

Mill, John Stuart. 1989. *'On Liberty' and Other Writings*, ed. Stefan Collini. Cambridge: Cambridge University Press.

Pettit, Philip. 2012. *On the People's Terms: A Republican Theory and Model of Democracy*. Cambridge: Cambridge University Press.

Rawls, John. 1999. *A Theory of Justice*, revised ed. Cambridge, MA: Belknap.

Rawls, John. 2005. *Political Liberalism*, expanded ed. New York: Columbia University Press.

Ripstein, Arthur. 2009. *Force and Freedom: Kant's Legal and Political Philosophy*. Cambridge, MA: Harvard University Press.

Simmons, A. John. 1979. *Moral Principles and Political Obligations*. Princeton: Princeton University Press.

Simmons, A. John. 1992. *The Lockean Theory of Rights*. Princeton: Princeton University Press.

Spooner, Lysander. 1882. *Natural Law: Or, the Science of Justice*. Boston: A. Williams and Co.

Stilz, Anna. 2009. *Liberal Loyalty: Freedom, Obligation, and the State*. Princeton: Princeton University Press.

Tomasi, John. 2012. *Free Market Fairness*. Princeton: Princeton University Press.

Vallier, Kevin. 2018. *Must Politics Be War? Restoring Our Trust in the Open Society*. New York: Oxford University Press.

Van der Vossen, Bas. 2015. "Imposing Duties and Original Appropriation", *Journal of Political Philosophy* 23 (1): 64–85.

Van der Vossen, Bas. 2020. "As Good as 'Enough, and as Good'", *Philosophical Quarterly* (online first).

Wiking, Meik. 2016, January 20. "Why Danes Happily Pay High Rates of Taxes", *U.S. News and World Report* (online).

First Round of Replies

Chapter 3

A Reply to Layman on Legitimacy and Disobedience

Michael Huemer

Contents

I The Case for Legitimacy

I would like to start by thanking Daniel Layman for his very interesting and thoughtful discussion of the case for political authority. Space limitations prevent me from discussing all aspects of Layman's chapter. In this chapter, I will focus on two things: (i) Layman's defense of political legitimacy and (ii) Layman's view of civil disobedience. In this section, I'm going to restate Layman's central argument for political legitimacy as I understood it (Layman may need to correct me if I have misunderstood it). In Sections 2–4, I will explain my main objections to that argument. In Section 5, I will discuss civil disobedience.

Let us start with the question of political legitimacy, then: Why may the state coercively impose its rules on the rest of society? As far as I understood it, Layman's argument, in outline, goes like this:

1. In the absence of government, we would necessarily suffer pervasive rights-violations. This is because:

DOI: 10.4324/9780429328046-6

a. Our rights are violated whenever our ability to exercise those rights depends upon the unaccountable will of others. (Layman refers to this kind of violation as "vitiation.")

b. In order for the exercise of our rights to not be subject to the unaccountable will of others, there must be institutions that define and enforce our rights, that resolve disputes concerning them, and that are equally accountable to all of us.

c. Private (nongovernmental) organizations could not do this. In particular, for-profit businesses could not be equally accountable to all of us because (i) wealth is very unequally distributed and (ii) for-profit businesses are inevitably controlled by those with more wealth.

2. Democratic government can solve this problem. This is because:

a. (Some) democratic governments effectively define and enforce rights and resolve disputes concerning them.

b. (Some) democratic governments are at the same time equally accountable to all citizens.

3. If some form of government can avoid pervasive rights-violations, and there is no nongovernment alternative that can do so, then that form of government is legitimate.

4. Therefore, (some) democratic governments are legitimate.

A few clarifications: In 2a, I inserted "(Some)" because I take it that not *all* democratic governments are effective at protecting rights, and I doubt that Layman thinks they are. Rather, I take it that Layman would point to certain high-quality democracies – including the United States, the United Kingdom, Canada, France, and so on – as showing how democratic governments at least *can* be reasonably effective and accountable to their people. Hereafter, let us assume that we are speaking of such relatively high-quality democracies. (But note that we are *not* speaking of any purely *hypothetical* form of government.) Accordingly, I take the conclusion (4) to entail that at least the existing, relatively high-quality democracies, such as the United States, France, Germany, and so on, are legitimate.

In 1a, 1b, 1c, and 2b, the notion of "accountability" appears. (In Layman's text, premises like 1a are initially expressed in terms of the "arbitrary" will of others. I assume that by "arbitrary," Layman means "unaccountable." That is necessary to fit with the rest of the argument.) For an organization to be "accountable" to us, we must have rights against that organization that we can insist on, and there must be institutions that will effectively support us in pressing those claims.

In brief: We all have certain rights – the right to property, the right not to be subject to unprovoked violence, etc. We also have a right to live in a society with institutions that protect those rights and to have an effective way of holding those institutions accountable for doing their job. Without a government, there would be no such institutions. It is only in a democracy that we can hold the government accountable. That is, very briefly and roughly, how I understand Layman's case for the legitimacy of democratic government.

2 Government Cannot Solve Layman's Problem

2.1 Layman's Condition Is Impossible

I'm afraid that I remain unconvinced by Layman's argument. I think premise 2 is false; I do not see how government could be said to solve the problem Layman sets up.

In Layman's view, our rights are "vitiated" whenever their enforcement "turns on nothing more than the judgments and preferences of those best able to enforce their wills."[1] But that condition obtains in all possible societies; indeed, that is almost a truth of logic.

To see my point, imagine a society with two people, Bart and Homer. Assume that Homer is the one better able to enforce his will. Then, *by definition*, if Homer tries to impose his will on Bart, Homer will (probably) succeed. In particular, if Homer decides to violate Bart's rights, Homer will (probably) succeed in doing so. Therefore, even if Homer always conscientiously chooses to respect Bart's rights, it will still be true that Bart's ability to enjoy his rights without infringement *depends upon* Homer's not deciding to violate them. And that decision on Homer's part will presumably be based on Homer's judgments and preferences. Therefore, Bart's enjoyment of his rights depends on the judgments and preferences of the person better able to enforce his will. Now, having seen that, it should be relatively easy to extend the point to societies in general.

---

1. See Layman's opening statement, this book, Chapter 2, Section 5, p. 80.

Nothing about government alters that basic logic. A governmental structure can't alter the logical truth that those who are best able to impose their will are most likely to succeed in doing so if they try. All that a form of government can accomplish is to alter *who* is best able to enforce their will: the establishment of a government gives *the members of that government* a much greater ability to impose their will, with a correspondingly lower ability for those outside the government. That's all.

What is the alternative supposed to be? Maybe the alternative would be that our rights are always enforced regardless of anyone's judgments or preferences? No, that's impossible. Rights won't enforce themselves. *Someone* has to do the enforcing. Whoever that is, they must have a superior ability to impose their will; otherwise, they will not be able to enforce anything. And the enforcer's actions will presumably depend upon the enforcer's judgments and preferences because that is how *all* human action is determined.

Perhaps the idea is that rights might be enforced not by a *person*, but by an *institution*, and an institution might be designed with rules and procedures that *require* the enforcement of rights. But this, again, is not a genuine alternative to dependence on "those best able to impose their will." The word "institution" does not refer to a special type of agent with no preferences or judgments, able to act autonomously from humans. The behavior of an institution is 100% dependent on the behavior of the individual *people* who staff that institution. And again, the behavior of people, in general, depends on those people's judgments and preferences. The creation of rules and procedures does not alter these facts. Rules and procedures cannot implement themselves; individual human beings must decide whether to follow them or not and then decide how they apply to a particular case. Thus, even if rights are enforced by an institution with rules and procedures, the enforcement of rights still depends on the judgments and preferences of particular people. If we rely on government for enforcement, then the security of our rights depends on the judgments and preferences of government officials, who are the ones best able to impose their will. So our rights are still inevitably vitiated.

Or perhaps the idea is that our rights are only vitiated when their enforcement depends upon some *individual*. The alternative would be that enforcement depends upon decisions of *many* people so that no one person could veto enforcement of your rights. Now, this is, in fact, an improvement in practical terms since a single person is more likely to make capricious judgments than a large group of people. And as long as we have a nondictatorial government, this condition is satisfied: no one person has the ability to decide to violate your rights, although a group of people (e.g., the legislature) can do so.

But if that is all we want, it is unclear why we need a government. Suppose that there were multiple competing rights-protecting agencies, each offering protection for a fee. In this case, again, there is no *one person* on whom the security of your rights depends. By the way, under the governmental system, but not the competitive market system, there is a single *organization* on whom the security of your rights depends and that you are born subject to. So if anything, the governmental system leaves your rights more dependent on caprice.

Maybe the idea is that a democratic government leaves the enforcement of our rights dependent on *us*, the voters, because we collectively have ultimate control over the government. But it is unclear how this would be an improvement over the preceding suggestion. No individual can control the mass of voters, so from each individual's perspective, the protection of one's rights depends upon the decisions of *other people*. If that should vitiate our rights, it does so whether the other people are government officials or our neighbors. It is also unclear how this would be an improvement over a market-based solution: private businesses are indirectly controlled by their customers, just as democratic governments are indirectly controlled by their constituents.

One final suggestion: perhaps the idea is that we could avoid the dependence on "those best able to impose their will" by establishing a society in which everyone has an *equal* ability (or inability) to impose their will. I shall discuss this in the next subsection.

2.2 We Are Not All Equal

The notion of *equality* plays a prominent role in Layman's arguments: the government must be *equally* accountable to all of us. It is this equality condition that is supposed to render anarcho-capitalism unacceptable – in Layman's view, we cannot rely on private companies to protect our rights because private companies are more responsive to those with greater economic power.

But this equality condition is no better satisfied by a democratic government than by a private corporation. By turning to government, we merely substitute *political* power for *economic* power. And political power, like economic power, is highly unequally distributed. If you doubt this, try calculating the odds that, in a country of over 300 million people, one recent President would happen to be the *son* of a previous President, that a recent Presidential candidate would happen to be the *brother* of one former President and son of another, and that another major Presidential candidate in the same year would happen to be the *wife* of a previous President.[2] If everyone has an equal chance to succeed in the political sphere, this is quite the coincidence.

Political power in the United States and other modern democracies is largely controlled by organized political parties. To attain political power, one must generally either have connections with party insiders, or at least an enormous amount of money. In the 2020 U.S. Presidential campaign, there were at least 21 millionaire candidates, including three billionaires, and only a few nonmillionaires. The average candidate had a net worth over $12 million.[3] Now, my point here is not to criticize these candidates for being wealthy. My point is simply that we do not all have an equal chance to exert political power. Indeed, it is far from clear that the political sphere is any more egalitarian than the economic sphere.

Moreover, it is also far from clear how equality should be thought to mitigate the problem of rights vitiation even if there were rough equality of political power. If the problem is that we must depend upon the will of others for our rights to be respected, how is it an improvement to say that we must depend upon the whims of masses of ordinary people, rather than the whims of a smaller (but still large) group of elites?

2.3 Government Is Unaccountable

You might think the preceding considerations simply show that Layman's condition for political legitimacy is too strict (or perhaps I have misunderstood it): It is too much to expect that the protection

---

2. I refer to George W. Bush (son of George H.W. Bush), Jeb Bush (brother of George W. Bush), and Hilary Clinton (wife of Bill Clinton).
3. Billionaires: Michael Bloomberg, Tom Steyer, Donald Trump. Mere millionaires, in descending order of wealth: John Delaney, Bill Weld, Michael Bennet, Elizabeth Warren, Joe Biden, Kamala Harris, Joe Sestak, Beto O'Rourke, Bill de Blasio, Bernie Sanders, Jay Inslee, Amy Klobuchar, Cory Booker, Steve Bullock, Marianne Williamson, Kirsten Gillibrand, Seth Moulton, Andrew Yang. Sources: Wolf 2020; Alexander et al. 2019.

of our rights should not depend on other people's judgments and preferences at all. Perhaps it is enough that we have institutions that are in fact reasonably reliable at protecting rights and that can be held accountable for doing so. Layman speaks at length about the importance of "accountability." Now, if we demand that this accountability should be independent of the preferences and judgments of other people, then we will be landed in the same problem we just discussed. But perhaps it is enough that there be mechanisms of accountability that, despite their inevitable reliance on the judgments and desires of people, are, in fact, reasonably reliable at holding government officials accountable.

What is accountability? Layman gives this helpful analogy: If students have a right to fair grading, then there should be some procedure by which students could complain about unfair grades, have their complaints fairly adjudicated by someone other than the professor who gave the grade, and receive some sort of remedy in the event that a grade is found to be unfair. If there are no such mechanisms, then, even if all professors are, in fact, grading fairly, the students' right to fair grading is not properly respected because professors are *not accountable*.

All this sounds to me reasonable and in line with the ordinary notion of "accountability." I agree, furthermore, that accountability is important and something we should want from our fundamental social institutions. Unfortunately, institutions such as the U.S. government are clearly *not accountable* in that sense. For the government to be accountable to you, there would have to be an institution to which you could complain if the government does not fulfill its duties to you, and that institution would have to be disposed, with at least a reasonable degree of reliability, to compel the government fulfill its duties or make amends for its failure to do so. Now, the central duties of the government, in Layman's view, include defining rights, enforcing rights, and fairly adjudicating disputes. So, for the government to be "accountable" to you, there must be some way that you can hold the government to account if it fails to adequately protect your rights or fairly resolve a dispute involving you.

There have, in fact, been many occasions on which the government has failed to adequately fulfill those duties, on *any* reasonable interpretation. I will give two sorts of examples. First example: you hear someone breaking into your house downstairs. You and your roommate call the police. The police dispatcher promises to send someone over. A police car then drives up to your house, looks at it briefly, then drives away. You call the police again. The dispatcher promises to send someone over again, but he, in fact, never sends anyone. As a result of this, you and your roommate wind up being beaten, robbed, and raped by the men who have broken into your house.

Second example: your wife is murdered in your house one morning while you are at work. The police quickly leap to the conclusion that *you* are probably the killer, and they conduct a shoddy investigation focused on coming up with reasons to blame you for the murder. They come across several pieces of evidence that point to your innocence, but they ignore this evidence. For instance, a witness reports having seen a strange van parked behind the house that morning, they find fingerprints on your house's sliding glass door that don't match anyone living in the house, they learn that your wife's credit card was used by an unknown person at a store 80 miles away two days after the murder, and so on. The prosecutor is legally required to turn over all this evidence to your lawyer; nevertheless, the prosecutor illegally suppresses the evidence, so you and your lawyer are unaware of it at the time of your trial. As a result, you are wrongfully convicted. You wind up spending 25 years in prison before the real killer is finally found.

The preceding cases are not fictional stories. They are actual cases from the annals of American law.[4] On any reasonable view, those qualify as cases in which the government culpably failed in its duties to the individual. In the first case, it failed to enforce your rights; in the second case, it failed to fairly adjudicate a dispute. Neither of these failures was understandable or excusable; both were clearly negligent if not malicious. Now, if one of these things happened to you, what recourse would you have to hold the government accountable for its failure?

There is, of course, no one for you to complain to but the government itself. You might wonder how fair it is, if you have a complaint against the government, for that same government to be the one to resolve that complaint. But suppose you complain to the government anyway. You try filing a lawsuit, in a government court,

---

4. The first story is the case of *Warren v. District of Columbia*, 444 A.2d. 1 (D.C. Ct. of Ap. 1981), which I mentioned in chapter 1. The second is the case of Michael Morton, described in Colloff 2012a, 2012b.

asking for some sort of redress for the harm that you suffered due to the government's failure to fulfill its duties. What will happen?

We don't have to guess, because several actual court cases have answered this already. The answer is that your lawsuit will be *summarily dismissed*. In other words, a judge will refuse to allow a trial, on the grounds that even if all your claims are factually correct, the government still owes you nothing. Why? In the first case (where you complain that the police failed to protect you), the judge will say you have no legitimate complaint because "a government and its agents are under no general duty to provide public services, such as police protection, to any particular individual citizen."[5] In the second case, where you complain that the prosecutor suppressed exculpatory evidence at your trial, your case will be dismissed because – even though the prosecutor clearly broke the law – prosecutors enjoy *absolute immunity* from lawsuits for misconduct committed while prosecuting a case.[6] (Judges, by the way, have also granted a parallel absolute immunity to themselves.)

What if other government officials – say, the legislature or the President – violate the law? Would you have any way of holding them accountable for that? Again, we don't have to guess because that has actually happened many times. Legislatures have often passed unconstitutional laws. Though these laws are occasionally struck down by courts, the legislators responsible for violating the constitution are never punished for doing so, no matter how clear and deliberate the violation may have been. No other government officials are ever punished for violating the constitution either.

Government officials have also sometimes violated statutory law. For example, there was the illegal burglary, obstruction of justice, and bribery ordered by President Richard Nixon; the illegal torture carried out by the Bush administration; and the illegal drone assassination program carried out by the Obama administration and

---

5. *Warren v. District of Columbia*, 444 A.2d 1 (1981), at p. 3. The Appeals Court approvingly quoted this phrase from the trial court's opinion. See also *Riss v. New York*, 22 N.Y.2d 579 (N.Y. 1968); *Hartzler v. City of San Jose*, 46 Cal.App. 3d 6 (1975); *DeShaney v. Winnebago County Department of Social Services*, 489 U.S. 189 (1989). These are all cases in which government courts refused to hold the government responsible for clear negligence, on the ground that the government has no duty to protect individuals.

6. *Imbler v. Pachtman*, 424 U.S. 409 (1976).

continued under the Trump administration. None of these presidents were ever legally punished for these crimes; in the latter two cases (torture and assassination), no one at all was ever punished.

What is my point with all this? To be clear, my point is not just that the government has done some bad things. My point is that the government *is not accountable*. Our institutional structure, in fact, does *not* include any effective mechanism for us to hold the government to account when it fails to do its job. The government decides what it wants to do. If it doesn't want to protect your rights, if it wants to violate your rights, or even if it wants to violate its own laws, it proceeds with impunity.

In summary, the problem Layman sets out is that we need our rights to be protected; this protection should not depend upon the desires and judgments of whoever is strongest, and whoever is responsible for protecting our rights should be accountable to us. This problem is not addressed by government. Government merely creates a particular group of people who are the strongest, who then impose their will on the rest of society. Democracy, again, does not change this situation; it merely alters who will be the strongest, and it makes our rights dependent on a larger group of potentially capricious others. Even democratic governments such as that of the United States are rarely accountable either: When they fail to perform their duties, there is no institution to whom one can complain other than the government itself, and that government routinely exempts itself from punishment or liability for its own failures. Since government does not, in fact, solve the problem of our rights being vitiated, this cannot provide a basis for political legitimacy.

3   Private Companies Fare Better Than the State

I turn now to my second objection to Layman's argument. Recall that Layman considers an alternative to government known as "anarcho-capitalism." Anarcho-capitalism is a possible social system in which protection would be provided by competing, private security guard companies rather than by a centralized, governmental police force, and disputes would be resolved by competing, private arbitration companies rather than by a centralized, governmental court system. There is no way of doing justice to the theory of anarcho-capitalism here, which is why I have not mentioned it before now. (In my experience, almost everyone thinks that they can easily refute this theory inside of 30 seconds, while actually having no idea what they're talking about because they've never read anything about it. If you're in that situation, go read a book on the subject.)[7]

I mention anarcho-capitalism now because Layman has argued that anarcho-capitalism could not avoid the problem of our rights being vitiated. Now, I agree that anarcho-capitalism could not fully solve this alleged problem, because no social system could do so. Again, no social system can avoid the problem that protection of our rights depends on other people's judgments and desires.

However, some social systems could at least have a reasonable degree of *accountability* for their basic institutions It happens that governmental systems do not, but it's plausible that an anarcho-capitalist system could be more accountable than a democratic government. In that sense, anarcho-capitalism would come closer to solving Layman's central problem than a democratic government does.

Why do I say that? First, some background about how I think about our society. Our society has two central mechanisms for providing services and distributing resources: its political mechanism (democracy) and its economic mechanism (the market). Anarcho-capitalism is a proposal to shift certain key services away from *democratic* control, to *market* control. Now, both of these mechanisms, for better or worse, are responsive to the beliefs and desires of the people, but they respond in different ways. We control democratic outcomes through *voting* decisions; we control market outcomes through *purchasing* decisions. In both cases, individuals seem powerless to change large-scale outcomes; only a movement of large numbers of people can change how the government/market behaves.

There are two key differences between the two control mechanisms. The first key difference is that in the market mechanism, unlike the democratic mechanism, an individual can make an effective decision for himself, by himself. In other words, when faced with different products, you can unilaterally decide that you want this product rather than that, and when you make that decision,

---

7. See, e.g., Friedman 1989; Rothbard 1978; Huemer 2013, Part 2.

you actually get the one that you chose. Or you can decide that you don't want any product of a given kind at all, in which case you don't get one, and you don't bear the cost either. For instance, if I am considering buying a car, I could decide that I don't want one, in which case I don't get a car and I don't pay the cost of one either. Or I could decide to buy a Honda, in which case I get a Honda (along with paying the cost of it).

By contrast, in the political system, no voter can unilaterally make any effective decisions. When faced with a collection of political candidates, you may decide that you don't want any of them and thus may refuse to vote for any of them. But you will wind up getting one of them anyway, along with whatever costs come with that candidate. Or you may decide to vote for candidate A over B, but that will not cause you to actually get A as your representative; you will still get whomever the majority of people vote for, which will be unaffected by your vote (except in the incredibly unlikely event that the other voters are exactly tied).

This key difference makes the market mechanism *more respon-sive* than the democratic mechanism. To begin with, since everyone knows that their vote will almost certainly never make any difference to the outcome of any election, voters typically put approximately zero effort into learning about the issues or forming reasonable opinions about them. Why waste your time doing research when you're just going to wind up with whatever the majority of your ignorant neighbors select anyway? Many surveys have confirmed the astounding ignorance of average voters. For instance, most Americans do not even know their Congressman's *name*, let alone his voting record. Most cannot name the three branches of their government or even the general *form* of government that they live under.[8] I mention these things because they more or less represent the least that one could possibly know about politics. By contrast, consumers usually at least put more effort into their purchasing decisions since that effort will actually affect what product they wind up with. (Most consumers, e.g., know whether they are buying a car or a turnip.)

---

8. Caplan 2007, p. 8; Rozansky 2014; Berry et al. 2009. For a bracing survey of voter ignorance, see Somin 2013, Chapter 1.

The problem: It is hard to see how voters could be said to hold their leaders *accountable* in any meaningful sense if the voters have no idea what their leaders are doing at any given time. The market mechanism, though still flawed, provides relatively more accountability, since consumers are more likely to know some of the relevant facts about the products that they buy.

The second key difference between market and government provision is that in the market, there usually are multiple, *competing* providers of a good or service. Government services, by contrast, are monopolistic (provided by a single entity). One result of this is that consumers are more likely to be *aware* of mistakes and failures by a particular company since they can contrast a bad company with other companies that do not make the same mistakes. A related consequence is that serious failures are likely to be costly for a business since consumers will switch to a competing provider.

Now, one might argue that there is also competition among governments: If your government is particularly awful, you can flee the country and thus obtain a new government. However, this is extremely costly and difficult. All or most other nations have immigration restrictions, so there may not, in fact, be any other country to which you can legally move. If you do move, you have to leave behind your family, your friends, your job, and your culture, all just to avoid buying a service from this one provider (the government). The market is not like that. If you don't like your cell phone provider, you don't have to abandon your family, friends, culture, and job just to switch phone providers. This difference has a predictable result: The market is much more responsive to consumer desires than the government is to citizen desires. To put the point in terms of accountability, the market provides a far more effective mechanism of accountability because there is a much *lower cost* of exercising the mechanism. (The mechanism is that, if a business does a poor job, you switch to one their competitors.)

Rather than relying on competition between different countries, you might try arguing that there is competition in a democratic state between different *political candidates*. Thus, you can hold government accountable by switching your vote to a different politician or party. This mechanism, however, is much less effective than the market mechanism for a couple of reasons. First, as we have noted earlier, switching your *vote* does not result in your actually *getting* a different political leader. Second, it is often difficult to tell what politician, if any, is responsible for a given outcome. If the economy goes into recession, is that because of the Republican President? Or the Democratic House? Or the unelected Federal Reserve? Or was it due to completely nongovernmental causes? One could do extensive research to try to figure this out, but there is no point in doing so because (see the first point again) you'll still get whatever politicians the majority of other people vote for.

As a result of all this, government failures often have the opposite effect on the government that business failures have on a business. Let's suppose that you own a store and you've hired a security guard company to watch over the store at night. You've just learned that there has been a major break-in at the store, thousands of dollars of merchandise was stolen, and the store is in shambles. Now, what would happen to the security guard company that you hired? You would probably fire them and switch to another company that does a better job of protecting their customers.

Now, for a contrast, suppose that you have a local government that provides security in your town through its police force. You've just learned that a major crime wave has started in your town. Houses and businesses are being vandalized, property is being stolen, and so on. What would happen to the police force? The answer is the opposite of the previous story: They would not be fired; they would receive *more money* to better combat crime. We can't fire them and go with their competitor because there is no competitor; government is by definition monopolistic. So, all we can do is give them more money and hope that causes them to do a better job.

Notice the incentive structure. If a private business fails at its central job, it *loses* money. If a government entity fails at its central job, it *gains* money and power. That's why private businesses tend to do a better job than governments. The market holds businesses accountable for their failures, in a way that the political process does not hold government accountable. Indeed, the political process does the precise opposite of holding government accountable: it *rewards* them for their failures.

Here is my favorite real-world illustration. On September 11, 2001, the United States suffered the worst terrorist attack in world history. The Pentagon was damaged and the World Trade Center was destroyed, at the cost of about 3,000 lives. Now, the entity responsible for protecting Americans from such attacks is the U.S. government. More specifically, the executive branch of the government. The head of the executive branch at the time was President George W. Bush. Therefore, if *anyone* should have taken a hit for failure to protect America, one would think that it would have been George W. Bush. Yet Bush suffered no political cost at all. Quite the contrary: immediately after the attack, President Bush's approval rating soared to 90%, the highest Presidential approval rating in history. There is a good chance that Bush wouldn't have won reelection in 2004 if not for the boost he gained from the terrorist attack. So, voters did not hold Bush accountable for failure to fulfill his central responsibility; they did just the opposite.

You might dispute whether Bush really deserved blame for his failure to protect America. It's a difficult job, it is hard to anticipate every threat, no attack of this kind had occurred before, etc. Fair points. But in the market, when a company gets bad results, you don't have to figure out whose fault it is. You just switch to another company. You don't care whether that's fair to the company or not; you just want the best results. The mechanism of market competition is harsh and unforgiving in that way. That is also why it does a far better job of holding people accountable.

4 Protection of Rights Provides No Basis for Legitimacy

At the outset, I formulated Layman's argument for political legitimacy as follows:

1. In the absence of government, we would necessarily suffer pervasive rights-violations.
2. Democratic government can solve this problem.
3. If some form of government can avoid pervasive rights-violations and there is no nongovernment alternative that can do so, then that form of government is legitimate.
4. Therefore, (some) democratic governments are legitimate.

In the preceding two sections, I have rebutted premises 1 and 2. In this section, I will also reject premise 3. I have two reasons for rejecting premise 3: the premise overlooks the fact that rights function as moral *constraints*, and it fails to provide a basis for *content independence*.

4.1   Rights as Constraints

Moral philosophers sometimes describe rights as **agent-centered constraints**.[9] What this means is that when you take account of the rights of others, your duty is not simply to reduce the total number of rights violations that occur in the world; your duty is to ensure that *you yourself* do not violate any rights. Thus, you may not violate another person's rights even if doing so would somehow prevent two other people from violating rights in a comparably serious way.

For example, let's suppose that you are the sheriff in a town where people are very angry about a particular recent crime. Crowds are demanding that someone to be punished. If no one is punished, there will be riots, during which multiple people will most likely be unjustly injured and possibly killed. Unfortunately, you are unable to find the criminal. What you *can* do, however, is to frame an innocent person, which will cause the innocent person to be punished but will also mollify the crowds and forestall the riots. Should you frame the innocent person?[10]

Almost everyone agrees that the answer is "no." But why not? The harm to the one innocent person would be less than the total harm expected from the riots. Furthermore, although people certainly have a right not to be unjustly punished, they also have a right not to be injured by rampaging mobs. As the sheriff, protecting the town from such riots is part of your responsibility; indeed, perhaps the town has a *right* to your protection.

This example illustrates the earlier point about agent-centered constraints: Your first duty is to avoid violating rights yourself. It is only *within that constraint* that you must try to protect people from having their rights violated by others.

Incidentally, there may be some limits to this. If violating one person's rights is somehow necessary to prevent World War III, then you should go ahead and violate the one person's rights. But at least in normal circumstances, you should not violate anyone's rights, even to prevent a greater number of comparable rights-violations by others.

---

9. On rights as moral constraints, see Nozick 1974, pp. 28–35. On agent-centeredness, see Scheffler 1994.
10. This example is from McCloskey 1957.

Having made that point, let us return to the argument for the state. The problem that we started out with is that the state frequently engages in behavior that would be considered rights-violations if any-one else were to do it. An account of legitimacy must explain why that behavior is not in fact morally wrong on the part of the state. Lay-man's argument offers us this answer: It is morally okay because the state has to do these things in order to protect our rights from other people (criminals, hostile foreign states). But this sounds like just the kind of tradeoff that we just rejected: it is not okay to violate some-one's rights even if doing so prevents someone else from violating two people's rights. Thus, *even if* government coercion were necessary to protect our rights, this would not be enough to make the govern-ment's coercion permissible. It therefore seems that premise 3 is false.

4.2 *Against Content Independence*

Some people would disagree with my point about rights mentioned earlier. Maybe the government's coercion is needed to prevent *so many* serious rights-violations that it is permissible for the gov-ernment to coerce us in ways that would normally be considered wrong. But even if you think that, surely this would only justify the acts of coercion that are *necessary* to prevent our rights from being violated in other ways. It wouldn't justify any *additional* coercive acts that are not part of protecting our rights. My illustration of this from Chapter 1 (Section 5.2): If you save the lifeboat from sinking by forcing people to bail water out of the boat, that does not mean that you can now go on to take the other passengers' money, stop them from eating potato chips, force them to pray to Poseidon, or throw overboard a passenger whom you don't like the looks of.

Layman hopes to get around this by appealing to "reasonable disagreement" about the function of government. In essence, Lay-man holds that whenever there is a reasonable disagreement about whether it is proper for the government to regulate something, it is permissible for the government to regulate that thing. He also thinks there is an enormous range of such reasonable disagreement. For example, he says that there is reasonable disagreement about whether the government should regulate pharmaceuticals; therefore, it is permissible for the government to regulate pharmaceuticals.

I am unconvinced. To begin with, I don't see why reasonable dis-agreement cuts in favor of government power, rather than against it. When the government "regulates" something, what this means is that the government issues commands, then sends armed guards to enforce those commands, typically by either kidnaping anyone who disobeys and locking them in a cage, or at least forcibly taking their money. Actions of that kind – kidnapping, theft, extortion – require a clear and powerful justification. The *presumption* is that they are *impermissible*, not permissible. To show a law to be permissible, you need something a lot better than, "Well, reasonable people disagree about whether this is a good idea." You need a *compelling case* that *is* a good idea.

Now let's be clearer about what it is that there is supposed to be reasonable disagreement about. The justification of government is supposed to be that government is necessary to define our rights, enforce those rights, and adjudicate disputes fairly (addressing the three "state of nature defects" that Layman raises in Section 4). So to argue that government may permissibly regulate some sphere of life, one has to argue that its doing so is necessary for the government to fulfill one or more of those functions. But for the overwhelming majority of regulations, I think there is no reasonable case at all for that, nor does anyone try to justify them in that way in reality.

Take the case of FDA regulations of pharmaceuticals. The Food and Drug Administration has an extremely onerous process for drugs to be approved, and without FDA approval, it is illegal to buy or sell a drug. For example, if you are dying of cancer, you have 6 months to live, and you want to try some drug that hasn't been proven effective, the government will try to forcibly prevent you from getting that drug. What exactly is the reasonable argument that this is necessary to protect someone's rights? Whose rights would this plausibly be protecting?

Maybe Layman would agree with me about that case; I don't know. Here is what he says about FDA regulation:

> Those who accept that the government ought to license drugs reason that since we must be able to rely on safe and effective medicine in order to plan our lives – or, indeed, to even live our lives – as independent equals, the state has standing to legislate, execute, and judge with respect to the quality and safety of drugs and keep those that fail off the market.

There seem to be five claims either asserted or implied:

1. FDA regulation is necessary for us to have safe and effective medicine.

2. FDA regulation is necessary for us to plan our lives.
3. FDA regulation is necessary for us to live our lives.
4. FDA regulation is necessary for us to be independent.
5. FDA regulation is necessary for us to be equals.

I don't understand #2, 4, or 5. If the FDA didn't regulate drugs, how would that stop you from planning your life? Or from being independent? Or from having equal rights with everyone else?

I assume #3 is dependent on #1: we need FDA regulation because it allegedly saves lives by giving us safe and effective medicine.[11] But this is irrelevant. The point that needed to be argued was that FDA regulation is necessary for the government to fulfill its duties of (i) defining our rights, (ii) enforcing those rights, and (iii) fairly adjudicating disputes. And no one thinks that, not even the FDA. To claim that the FDA improves the quality of health care is just to make a completely different argument.

Perhaps Layman would say that we have a *right* to high-quality medical care – or at least that that is a reasonable view. And since that is a reasonable view, it is legitimate for the government to deploy coercion to try to improve the quality of medical care, including by prohibiting unproven drugs.

To test this moral reasoning, let's entertain an analogy. We're back on the lifeboat. You've just saved the lifeboat from sinking by forcing everyone to bail water. Now you notice a passenger who is sharing his potato chips with other passengers. You point out that potato chips are low-quality food, with too much saturated fat and acrylamide, but the passengers don't care; they go on eating.

If it's reasonable to think there is a right to high-quality health care, I suppose it is about equally reasonable to think there is a right to

---

11. No doubt some lives are saved because the FDA prevents people from taking some dangerous drugs. Some lives are also *lost* because the FDA prevents people from taking life-saving drugs. David Friedman (1989, p. 92) gives the example of the drug timolol, a beta blocker, which the FDA approved in 1981. At that time, timolol had already been widely used in other countries for over a decade. When the FDA finally approved it, they congratulated themselves, predicting that this decision would save 7,000–10,000 lives a year in the United States. The implication, however, was that during the preceding decade, the FDA had killed 70,000–100,000 Americans by prohibiting them from using this life-saving drug.

high-quality food. Now, just as the FDA claims to improve the quality of medicine by prohibiting what it considers bad (unsafe, ineffective, or unproven) medicines, you on the lifeboat might try to improve the quality of food by prohibiting what you consider bad (unhealthful) foods. Since there could be reasonable disagreement about the right to high-quality food, does this mean it is permissible for you to forcibly seize the chips to prevent anyone from eating them?

No, it doesn't. For one thing, even if people have a right to healthy food, it can't reasonably be claimed that this right is violated by people's voluntarily choosing to eat potato chips (would they be violating their own right?) This example shows that the conditions for ethically justifying coercion are much stricter than Layman recognizes. To justify coercion, it is not enough to cite some good that some people think we have a right to and claim that you are increasing the quality of that good.

5   Civil Disobedience

I turn to the topic of civil disobedience, the phenomenon in which citizens deliberately disobey the law because they believe the law to be unjust or otherwise wrong. Layman thinks that disobedience should be rare, it should be done openly and publicly, and the citizen must voluntarily accept legal punishment for disobeying the law. I disagree.

Think about the lifeboat story again. Suppose that you've seized the potato chips from one of the passengers, declaring that no one may eat potato chips, due to your need to protect everyone from saturated fat. Several of the passengers on the boat think, correctly, that you are behaving very badly and have no right to seize anyone's chips. One of them also happens to have another bag of chips hidden in his coat. He is afraid of you, though, due to your penchant for waving your gun around and making irrational demands. So, he takes the chips out surreptitiously and eats them in a corner of the boat while you aren't looking. You discover the passenger's disobedience when you find him holding an empty potato chip bag, with some potato crumbs on his shirt. You then demand that he submit to a beating, in punishment for his disobedience.

I have three questions about this story:

1. Was it morally wrong for the passenger to eat the chips secretly instead of doing it in front of your face?

2. Was it wrong of the passenger to eat the chips at all since he had only a minor interest in eating potato chips and you had a reasonable argument against potato-chip-eating?
3. Is the passenger morally obligated to submit to a beating from you?

These are easy questions. The answer is "no." I find the third question the most striking, so I shall focus on that question here: It is absurd to think that the passenger should submit to a beating. *You're* the one who acted reprehensibly in this story, so if anyone should be submitting to a beating, it should be you.

That is how I view civil disobedience. When the government has abused its power, and a citizen *rightly* disregards the government's immoral command (an act that, by the way, often involves great moral courage and commitment to justice), why would the blameless citizen agree to be punished by the agent who committed the only wrong in the story? That is the exact opposite of justice. That is akin to the idea that if I steal your wallet, *you* should apologize to *me*.

Layman thinks that citizens who disobey unjust laws have to accept punishment because

> to do otherwise would be to treat one's own will and judgment as sovereign over others, and that would disrespect them and their equal rights.[12]

I disagree with that. It's crucial to understand what Layman and I do *not* disagree about, though. We *agree* that *some* laws are unjust and that disobedience is *sometimes* justified. (For instance, the Fugitive Slave Laws in the 1800s were unjust, and individuals were justified in violating those laws, e.g., by helping slaves escape from their masters.) By stipulation, we're considering one of those cases where the law is wrong and disobedience is justified. So by hypothesis, the government had no right to make the law in question in the first place, which is to say that the government had no right to issue threats of punishment for people who disobey that law (passing a law just *is* issuing threats of punishment for

---

12. Layman, this book, Chapter 2, Section 8, p. 108.

people who behave in a particular way). For the same reason, citizens who support that law had no right to have such a law passed or enforced; one cannot have a right to have other people act unjustly and immorally. Therefore, evading enforcement of the law does not show disrespect for anyone's rights; it is only the *enforcement* of the unjust law that shows disrespect for rights. If someone is trying to violate your rights, you do not show disrespect for anyone's rights by trying to prevent the violation. To say otherwise is like claiming that one disrespects the rights of a mugger if one fails to hand over one's wallet.

Evading punishment also does not treat your will or judgment as sovereign over anyone. It merely refuses to treat others as sovereign over you. If someone is trying to abuse you, acting to prevent the abuse does not set you up as their master. It merely refuses to accept them as *your* master. Which is what any self-respecting person should do.

But even if I am wrong about that, and avoiding unjust punishment is somehow disrespectful to the people who are immorally trying to punish you, I still think that is a *trivial* consideration, vastly outweighed by your interest in avoiding wrongful punishment. Let me give another example to illustrate.

Let's start with an action that would *clearly* express *great* disrespect for another person. Suppose you go up to a neighbor and say, "You disgust me. I have no respect at all for you or your supposed 'rights'. You are inferior to me and fit only to serve me." Then you turn your back and walk away. In doing this, you would be expressing disrespect for the neighbor and his equal rights, *far* more clearly than you would by merely evading punishment for breaking a law. And, in normal circumstances, that would certainly be a bad thing to do.

But let's add to the story. Imagine that the *reason* you did this was that there is a group of terrorists who were going to kidnap you and hold you hostage for 5 years in dangerous, unsanitary, and terrifying conditions. The police can't stop them. You can't defend yourself from them. You can't run or hide from them. The *only* way you could avoid being taken prisoner by the terrorists was to give them what they want. And the only thing they want is for you to viciously insult your neighbor, as described earlier. (Just accept this odd scenario for the sake of argument.) *Now* what do we think about your action?

It doesn't seem so bad anymore. Sure, your neighbor will feel bent out of shape for a while. But big deal. That is *trivial* in comparison to the harm of 5 years of wrongful imprisonment. Your interest in avoiding kidnapping clearly outweighs the moral reason not to insult your neighbor.

Similarly, even if avoiding punishment for breaking a law is somehow disrespectful to others, that by itself is at most a trivial harm, which is *clearly* justified if it enables you to avoid being unjustly kidnapped and held prisoner by the state for multiple years.

Perhaps Layman would say that the civil disobedience case is worse because you are disrespecting everyone, not just one person. In that case, modify my example as follows: instead of just insulting your neighbor, imagine that you buy a billboard by the freeway and post the same message on it, to be viewed by thousands of motorists every day, clearly expressing disrespect for all your fellow citizens. Still, this rather annoying action would easily be justified if you had to do it to prevent yourself from being kidnaped and held prisoner for 5 years.

6 Summary

I have argued that Layman's case for political legitimacy fails because

1. Government does not prevent our rights from being vitiated. It merely makes our rights dependent on the unaccountable will of government officials and (mostly ignorant and irrational) voters.
2. Market mechanisms are more accountable than democratic mechanisms.
3. Even if government were needed to reduce rights-violations, this wouldn't justify the government in violating rights to achieve this result.
4. Nor would it justify the government in forcibly imposing policies that are not actually necessary to protect our rights.

In response to Layman's view of civil disobedience, I have argued that there is no reason to accept punishment for a justified act of disobedience to an unjust law. It is not disrespectful to prevent someone else from violating your rights. Even if it were, the trivial badness of expressing disrespect would easily be outweighed by the need to avoid a serious, tangible harm such as imprisonment.

References

Alexander, Dan, Chase Peterson-Withorn, and Michela Tindera. 2019, August 14. "The Net Worth of Every 2020 Presidential Candidate", *Forbes*. Retrieved July 30, 2020 from www.forbes.com/sites/danalexander/2019/08/14/heres-the-net-worth-of-every-2020-presidential-candidate/.

Berry, Mindy, ZeeAnn Mason, Scott Stephenson, and Annie Hsiao. 2009. *The American Revolution: Who Cares?* Philadelphia, PA: American Revolution Center.

Caplan, Bryan. 2007. *The Myth of the Rational Voter*. Princeton, NJ: Princeton University Press.

Colloff, Pamela. 2012a, November. "The Innocent Man, Part One", *Texas Monthly*. Retrieved June 25, 2019 from www.texasmonthly.com/politics/the-innocent-man-part-one/.

Colloff, Pamela. 2012b, December. "The Innocent Man, Part Two", *Texas Monthly*. Retrieved June 25, 2019 from www.texasmonthly.com/articles/the-innocent-man-part-two/.

Friedman, David. 1989. *The Machinery of Freedom*, 2nd ed. LaSalle, IL: Open Court.

Huemer, Michael. 2013. *The Problem of Political Authority*. New York: Palgrave Macmillan.

McCloskey, H. J. 1957. "An Examination of Restricted Utilitarianism", *Philosophical Review* 66: 466–485.

Nozick, Robert. 1974. *Anarchy, State, and Utopia*. New York: Basic Books.

Rothbard, Murray. 1978. *For a New Liberty*. Lanham, MD: University Press of America.

Rozansky, Michael. 2014, September 17. "Americans Know Surprisingly Little About Their Government, Survey Finds", *Annenberg Public Policy Center*. Retrieved November 15, 2018 from www.annenbergpublicpolicycenter.org/americans-know-surprisingly-little-about-their-government-survey-finds/.

Scheffler, Samuel. 1994. *The Rejection of Consequentialism*. Oxford: Clarendon.

Somin, Ilya. 2013. *Democracy and Political Ignorance*. Stanford, CA: Stanford University Press.

Wolf, Christopher. 2020, February 20. "How Rich Are the 2020 Presidential Candidates?", *U.S. News and World Report*. Retrieved July 30, 2020 from www.usnews.com/news/elections/articles/2020-02-20/the-net-worth-of-the-2020-presidential-candidates.

Chapter 4

Accountability, Methodology, and Respect

A Reply to Huemer

Daniel Layman

Contents

I How Equal Freedom Under Government Is Possible

Let me begin by thanking Mike Huemer for a characteristically clear, vigorous, and insightful reply to my opening chapter. His arguments in response to my own all merit focused attention, and I will respond to them in turn. In doing so, I will draw out what I take to be a methodological problem that underlies – and undercuts – much of his reasoning in both of his chapters so far.

It will be best, I think, to launch the argument of this chapter by considering a dilemma that Huemer poses for my standard of freedom from arbitrary power, which we may also call "nondomination." On the one hand, we might understand arbitrary power as the sheer, physical capacity to interfere with another person. If this is what arbitrary power amounts to, freedom from arbitrary power is impossible; people, after all, typically *can* interfere with anyone they encounter, including in ways that seriously invade rights. For example, if I pass you on the street, I *could* punch you in the face,

DOI: 10.4324/9780429328046-7

thus seriously invading several of your important rights. I would no doubt suffer serious consequences for doing so, but that makes no difference to whether I could do it. Since we cannot realistically live with others under conditions that make it impossible for people to interfere with one another, freedom from arbitrary power is an absurd standard of freedom.

On the other hand, we might understand arbitrary power as unaccountable power. On this understanding, I am subject to your arbitrary power within the scope of my rights to the extent that you are not accountable for respecting my rights. This framing of arbitrary power avoids setting an impossible standard; people, after all, can be and often are accountable to one another. Nevertheless, it sets a standard that all governments fail to meet. There are two reasons for this failure. First, governments are not accountable to most people; citizens frequently lack adequate recourse when their governments come up short on their obligations. For instance, American courts have ruled that police departments are not civilly liable for providing any particular service to any particular person but are instead accountable only for policing the community in general.[1] Second, when government is accountable to particular people, this typically turns on wealth, family connections, and so forth. The members of the Bush and Clinton families, for instance, have had astonishing success at placing themselves in the United States' highest offices. In short, governments are nearly always unaccountable, and any accountability to which they are subject is both (very) unequally distributed and based on wealth and connections. These failures of government accountability stand in stark contrast to the rigorous accountability that exists within markets. Since customers will abandon firms that fail to meet expectations, accountability is as prominent in markets as it is absent from government. Consequently, to the extent that I affirm accountability as essential to nondomination and so to rightful freedom, I should accept anarcho-capitalism rather than state authority.

I do not believe that my view faces this dilemma. Nevertheless, I am glad that Huemer has posed it because it provides a helpful framework not just for responding to his objections but also

---

1. *Warren v. District of Columbia*, 444 A.2d 1 (1981).

for clarifying and expanding the positions I staked out in my first chapter.

Let's begin with the relationship between arbitrary power and the sheer possibility of interference. Huemer rightly senses that I do not actually mean to endorse the view that people are unfree within their rights to the extent that it is physically possible for others to invade their rights at will. After detailing how silly it would be to suggest that morally significant freedom of any sort turns on such physical possibility, Huemer asks of my account: Does "arbitrary" mean the same thing as "unaccountable?" Not quite. "Arbitrary" means what its etymology suggests: "willful" in the sense of *merely* willful.[2] To be subject to another person's power is to be subject to her will simply as such – that is, *not* as situated within institutions that appropriately constrain it. Insofar as someone holds arbitrary power over me, "Because I said so!" is all the justification her actions towards me require. This rough-and-ready framing of arbitrary power, though helpful as a conceptual introduction, is hardly sufficient on its own. Before we can put it to use, we need a more particular conception that details what human relationships need to be like to avoid manifesting such power.[3] As we will shortly see, it is here, in the move from the core concept of accountability to an adequate conception of it, that accountability makes its appearance.

One influential conception of subjection to arbitrary power, which is suggested by certain passages in Philip Pettit's ground-breaking work on republican freedom, is that one person, A, is subject to the arbitrary power of another person, B, to the extent that it is *possible* for B to interfere with A in ways contrary to her avowed interests.[4] This is precisely the conception that Huemer has in mind when he argues that the absence of arbitrary power may be an impossibly utopian ideal. After all, arbitrary interference is widely possible (if not likely) within any kind of human society we can imagine. To borrow a now-classic example, it is always possible

---

2. 'Arbitrary' derives from the Latin '*arbitrium*,' which mean 'choice' or 'will'.
3. For the distinction between general concepts (e.g., "cruel punishment") and their particular conceptions, or interpretations (e.g., "severely painful punishment"), see Dworkin 1986, pp. 70–72.
4. For example, Pettit 1997, pp. 52–55.

that any person who happens to be physically located near both you and a water jug *could* grab the jug and smash you over the head with it.[5] If rightful freedom requires such interference to be impossible, then rightful freedom is itself impossible, with or without government.

I agree with Huemer here; any conception of nondomination that requires arbitrary interference to be impossible is unacceptable. To arrive at a more adequate conception of nondomination, we need to develop a conception of arbitrary power that captures the idea that nondomination is a matter of constraining others' wills without equating constraint with impossibility. That conception, I suggested in my first chapter, is arbitrary power as unaccountable power, with accountability conceptualized as follows: An agent, A, is accountable to another agent or group, B, to the extent that (1) A owes something to B; (2) B has standing to insist to A that A discharge her obligation; and (3) B can rely on institutional backup in support of her claim against A.[6] I do not claim, then, that governments must – or even can – render arbitrary interference within rights impossible. To the contrary, political authority depends on accountability. Government must secure a regime of equal basic accountability under law, which, in turn, requires democratic institutions of the kind I described in my first chapter.

In light of these commitments, we face the second horn of Huemer's dilemma: Do any governments actually secure accountability as I conceive of it? And, in any event, wouldn't anarcho-capitalism certainly secure it much more effectively? The answers to these questions are, respectively, a qualified 'yes' and an unqualified 'no.' Let's consider them in turn.

Huemer argues that actual governments are not accountable to their citizens, at least under ordinary circumstances. In support of this claim, he marshals myriad examples of government entities in the United States failing to protect or otherwise provide services to citizens who then have little or no recourse. Two such examples receive special attention. One of these is *Warren vs. District of Columbia*, in which District of Columbia Court of Appeals ruled that the police were not liable for the rape, assault, and robbery that resulted when

---

5. Gaus 2003, p. 70.
6. Layman, this book, Chapter 2, Section 5, p. 86.

they failed to investigate a home following a 911 call.[7] The other is prosecutors' immunity from civil liability for incompetence and misconduct even when it is egregious and results in wrongful conviction and imprisonment (as it sometimes does). Huemer notes, correctly, that decisions like *Warren* issue from courts and other governmental bodies with some regularity, not just in the United States, but in all nations. And he points out, again correctly, that prosecutorial immunity is hardly the only instance of a powerful state agent being either wholly or substantially protected from civil liability. Don't examples such as these show that actual governments are unaccountable and therefore illegitimate by my own standards?

The first thing to note in response is that as I argued earlier, legitimacy comes in degrees; it is not an all-or-nothing affair. So, even if state behavior of the sort Huemer highlights here damages legitimacy, that doesn't mean that it destroys it completely. Moreover, since, as I also argued earlier, our political obligations can survive a significant (though not unlimited) degree of illegitimacy, we may not move directly from the observation that some action by the state damages its legitimacy to the conclusion that its citizens have no obligation to obey it. Nevertheless, Huemer clearly means to argue that contemporary democracies are radically unaccountable in a way that eviscerates any defense of legitimacy that turns, as mine does, on accountability to the public. Consequently, we need to consider his argument in detail to determine whether it succeeds.

As I understand it, Huemer's argument against accountability-based state legitimacy proceeds as follows:

1. To the extent that a state is accountable in the sense that might make it legitimate, it is liable for the losses that particular citizens incur due to its behavior.
2. Actual states are rarely liable for the losses that particular citizens incur due to their behavior.
3. Therefore, actual states are rarely accountable in the sense that might make them legitimate.

The problem with this argument is that premise 1 turns on a confusion between (a) tortious liability of state actors and (b)

---

7. *Warren v. District of Columbia*, at p. 3.

democratic accountability. Tortious liability is an agent's susceptibility to lawsuits in the event that she (or it – some agents may not be natural persons) culpably, but non-criminally, harms another agent. For example, I am likely to be liable in this sense for injuries I cause you if I plow into your car while texting. Tortious liability is, to be sure, a kind of accountability; it is a way in which agents within a civil polity may force one another to internalize improperly imposed costs. Nevertheless, it is quite distinct from democratic accountability, which, as I argued in my first chapter, is the equal basic accountability of a political community's whole system of law and policy to its democratically represented people. In fact, one of the questions that such a system of law and policy must settle is the extent of tortious liability to which various actors, including state actors, will be subject.

Now, it is by no means the case that all answers to this question are equally just. Indeed, I am inclined to agree with Huemer that significantly limiting the tortious liability of state actors such as police officers and prosecutors is a very bad policy against which citizens should argue vigorously. But this does not mean that the state lacks equal basic accountability insofar as it enacts bad policy of this kind. To the contrary, if, as is often the case in the United States, much of the public is strongly committed to very low levels of liability for state actors such as the police, then the fact that our democratic apparatus secures such low levels of liability is evidence for the operation of equal basic accountability rather than evidence against it.

It is important to emphasize that I am not claiming that citizens should just meekly accept unjust policies like those that limit state actors' civil liability. We should protest such policies vigorously, and civil disobedience (which I discussed earlier and will shortly discuss again) may sometimes be appropriate in light of them. Nevertheless, unjust tort policy is simply not the same problem as an absence of equal basic accountability through the democratic process.

With this much in hand, let's now consider the other problem Huemer raises for my reliance on equal basic accountability. How, Huemer asks, is it compatible with legitimacy as I understand it for people like the Bushes, the Clintons, and the Trumps – or even just ordinary rich people – to have such an outsized likelihood of holding high political office and otherwise shaping policy? My answer is simple, and it is the same one I gave in my discussion of campaign finance in my first chapter: Such wealth and influence-based power over the state *is* incompatible with equal basic accountability and consequently damages legitimacy. That is, states infested with such power are less legitimate than they otherwise would be, and their citizens should demand better – loudly, repeatedly, and perhaps even disruptively. But this does not mean that such states are failed states and so unable to support political obligations. This would only be the case if their citizens stood a better chance of securing a legal regime of equal basic accountability by disbanding their political community and starting over than by working to fix the community they have. And, as I have argued, the United States and similarly flawed but basically functional democracies maintain levels of legitimacy well above this threshold.

At this point, though, Huemer has a rejoinder: Even if I'm right about equal basic accountability under merely flawed democracies, wouldn't anarcho-capitalism be more accountable still? Firms, after all, are directly accountable to customers for providing agreed-upon goods and services at agreed-upon prices. Consequently, if people purchased all of their goods and services – including those traditionally supplied by states, such as security – from private suppliers, poor service would all but guarantee lost business. Even if states significantly increased liability for public actors, it is not plausible that any state-to-citizen relationship could approximate the kind of direct and consequential individual accountability that characterizes the firm-to-customer relationship. Thus, even if equal basic accountability under government is something we possess to a considerable extent and upon which we may reasonably hope to improve, we could be sure of far greater accountability if we simply dispensed with government altogether.

The trouble with this view does not lie in the suggestion that anarcho-capitalist service providers would be more directly accountable to their customers than democracies are to particular citizens. If company X, which competes with companies Y and Z, agrees to sell me its Bronze Security Plan for $500 per month, it is, indeed, accountable for providing that plan at that price, as I will simply switch to Y or Z if it fails to do so. No move available to democratic citizens is relevantly analogous to taking one's business elsewhere. The problem, however, is that a vast web of private economic relationships, each of which might feature accountability of this sort, cannot constitute a community wherein all members relate to one another as free and equal rights-holders. This is because such a web is compatible with enormous levels of unaccountable power, not necessarily of particular firms over their customers, but rather of rich customers over poor customers (and, perhaps, of rich firms over poor firms and their customers). Under anarcho-capitalism, the rich, who would (as Huemer grants) be able to afford high-quality security, would be largely secure against the poor, but not vice versa. Moreover, since all law would be private and agreed upon by litigants or the firms representing them, relatively rich people would almost always be able to leverage their economic position for favorable legal terms in the event of judicial proceedings against relatively poor people. Anarcho-capitalism is thus necessarily and intrinsically rife with arbitrary power, which means that it necessarily and intrinsically supports rights vitiation on a massive scale. The *de facto* lordship of the rich is a feature of anarcho-capitalism, not a bug.

2   Rights as Constraints

I argued in my first chapter that the state is legitimate insofar as it defines, adjudicates, and enforces rights in a way that secures citizens against arbitrary power within the scope of their rights. According to Huemer, this amounts to saying that the state may violate people's rights in some cases – by taxing them, for instance – to secure fewer rights violations on the whole. He writes:

> The problem that we started out with is that the state frequently engages in behavior that would be considered rights-violations if anyone else were to do it. An account of legitimacy must explain why that behavior is not in fact morally wrong on the part of the state. Layman's argument offers us this answer: it is morally okay because the state has to do these things in order to protect our rights from other people (criminals, hostile foreign states).[8]

The reasoning he thus attributes to me is flawed, he claims, because it turns on a misunderstanding of rights and their moral demands. Rights, Huemer explains, are agent-centered constraints:

---

8. Huemer, this book, Chapter 3, Section 4, p. 133.

What this means is that when you take account of the rights of others, your duty is not simply to reduce the total number of rights violations that occur in the world; your duty is to ensure that *you yourself* do not violate any rights. Thus, you may not violate another person's rights even if doing so would somehow prevent two other people from violating rights in a comparably serious way.[9]

If rights are indeed agent-centered constraints, then it cannot be okay to defend rights-violations by the state on the grounds that those violations decrease rights violations overall. For, "*even if* government coercion were necessary to protect our rights, this would not be enough to make the government's coercion permissible."[10]

I agree with Huemer that rights are agent-centered constraints and that rights create duties of respect, not of maximization. A utilitarianism of rights, according to which people ought to act in whatever way minimizes rights violations, would badly misconstrue the purpose and character of rights. However, I do not believe, and I have not argued, that the state violates our rights by subjecting us to its coercive rule. To the contrary, I have argued that the state has a right to subject us to (properly structured) coercive rule because such rule is a necessary condition of us enjoying our rights at all. Since the state has a right to subject us to coercive rule, none of us has a right not to be subject to that rule, which, in turn, means that the state does not violate our rights by subjecting us to it.

An example will be helpful here. Each of us, I suppose, has a general right not to be pushed by passersby. This in turn means that passersby generally have a duty not to push us. But this does not entail that passersby never have a right to push us even if we grant that rights are agent-centered constraints. Most of us agree that if I will step on an unseen toddler unless you push me, you have right – and perhaps even a duty – to push me. This does not mean that you have a right to violate my right; for reasons Huemer has identified and I have affirmed, no one can have a right to violate any of my rights. Nor does it mean that rights are not really agent-centered constraints. Rather, it means that my right not to be pushed is always

9. Huemer, this book, Chapter 3, Section 4, p. 132.
10. Huemer, this book, Chapter 3, Section 4, p. 133.

conditional even if we don't often spell out the conditions. That is, my right not to be pushed is actually my right not to be pushed, *barring certain extenuating circumstances*. When those extenuating circumstances are present, I have no right not to be pushed, which means that you don't violate my rights by pushing me.

Allowing that the content of rights is conditional does not amount to an abandonment of the idea that rights are agent-centered constraints, let alone the affirmation of some kind of utilitarianism of rights. For, whereas the character of rights as agent-centered constraints concerns the *form* of rights, the conditionality of rights is a feature of the *content* of rights. Regardless of what it is we are entitled to as a matter of right, that entitlement is an agent-centered constraint. But this tells us nothing at all about how simple or complex any given rightful entitlement is, much less that all rightful entitlements are unconditional. A conditional right against being pushed except when certain extenuating circumstances are present is no less an agent-centered constraint than an unconditional right against being pushed by anyone, at any time, for any reason. Thus, whether rights are conditional or unconditional cannot be settled simply by appealing to the formal structure of rights as agent-centered constraints. To the contrary, we must do the substantive moral work of figuring out if (and when, why, and how) particular rights are conditional.

The case for understanding the right against being pushed as conditional is straightforward enough: If that right were unconditional, you would have a duty to refrain from pushing me to save a toddler, which would be crazy. Similar remarks apply to many of our everyday rights, including our property rights. Pretty much no one, for instance, thinks that my right to my lawn extends to pushing people off it and into the waiting jaws of a rabid dog in the street. What, though, about the state's right to subject us to an equally basically accountable legal regime? Why should we believe that the state has a right to rule even though most of the particular acts that constitute the state's rule (e.g., taxing and arresting) would violate our rights if they were done by anyone other than agents of the state? This question is no doubt a very important one. But it might strike you as strangely familiar. That is because it is just the basic question of political legitimacy with which we began this book! It is no good, then, to appeal to the form of rights as agent-centered constraints to reject a substantive account (such as my own) of the state's right to rule because doing so just leads us right back to where we started.

3   Anti-Exceptionalism and Begging the Question

I have just argued that we may not infer from the premise that rights are agent-centered constraints the conclusion that rights are substantively unconditional and so not subject to conditions that permit the state to rule. Huemer, however, might grant that rights as agent-centered constraints don't necessarily have to be unconditional. Rather, rights as agent-centered constraints must *either* be unconditional *or* have conditions that can in principle be met by state and non-state actors alike. If one claims (as I have done) that our rights have conditions that only states can meet, this claim must somehow break down into a failure to recognize fully what rights are and what kinds of duties they place on us.

Why, though, can't rights have conditions that only states can meet? After all, there is nothing incoherent about agent-centered constraints with state-specific conditions. It seems to me that Huemer's unwillingness to consider state-specific conditions on our rights results from a more basic commitment that underlies his entire argument: The state is justified in doing something only if there are, at least in principle, non-state actors who are justified in doing the same thing. Put another way, state action cannot be morally one-of-a-kind, or subject to norms that apply, as a matter of principle, only to the state as such. Let's call this principle **Anti-Exceptionalism**:

> **Anti-Exceptionalism:** Condition C justifies action A when performed by the state if, and only if, C justifies A when performed by anyone at all.

As you will recall, Huemer opens his first chapter with the example of a vigilante who takes it upon herself to round up and punish people who have been vandalizing her neighborhood, and to lock up anyone who refuses to support her antivandalism efforts financially. Nearly all of us, Huemer rightly notes, would object to this behavior. But isn't this the kind of thing that the state does all the time? And doesn't that mean that the state's behavior is also wrong? The argumentative force of this parable turns, in the first place, on the assumption that the vigilante and the state are doing the same thing. On some descriptions of what each party does, this is simply not true; the vigilante violently compels people to take part in a personal project, whereas the state enforces the law. But on a very reductive – indeed, physical – level of description, the vigilante and the state agent do carry out the same action, namely that of coercing and confining people who disobey rules. So, the challenge that issues from the example is: Why is it okay when the state coerces and confines people who disobey rules but wrong when the vigilante coerces and confines people who disobey rules? Huemer's point in emphasizing this and similar cases is that any satisfactory answer must identify some feature of the action as performed by the state that would serve to justify the vigilante's behavior if we suitably modified that behavior to include that feature. Any account of state legitimacy that cannot apply just as well to a suitably altered vigilante scenario violates Anti-Exceptionalism and therefore fails.

Anti-Exceptionalism is, perhaps, attractive at first glance. This is because it resembles (at least superficially) the very respectable principle that no defense of state authority (or of anything else, for that matter) should be *ad hoc* – that is, ginned up in an unprincipled fashion to shore up a foregone conclusion. A good example of an *ad hoc* justification is the one recently offered by U.S. Senate Republicans for their decision to confirm President Trump's nomination of Amy Coney Barrett to the Supreme Court. They happily conducted this confirmation during the final months of Trump's presidency despite having refused to hold hearings for Merrick Garland, whom President Obama appointed to the Court with nearly a year remaining in his presidency, supposedly on the grounds that the Senate should not consider Supreme Court nominees during election years. Nearly everyone agrees that the real explanation for the Republicans' choices was very simple; they saw levers of power, and they pulled them. Nevertheless, many of the senators who took part in this about-face offered the convoluted justification that it is okay to hold Supreme Court hearings during election years as long as the same party holds both the Presidency and the Senate majority. This explanation, it seems, was merely window dressing on a decision that rested on entirely unrelated grounds. In the context of the legitimacy debate, my claim that the state may jail people because it has a special kind of authority that non-state actors necessarily lack may seem a lot like the Senate Republicans' claim that they may confirm Barrett because the President and the Senate majority hail from the same party.

Accounts like mine, then, must show that they are not objectionably *ad hoc*, the philosophical equivalent of Senate Majority

Leader Mitch McConnel's tortuous rhetorical performances on the Senate floor. To avoid being thus *ad hoc*, a defense of state authority must be *principled*; it must show that there is a moral principle that explains the state's special standing. But Anti-Exceptionalism does not merely demand that a successful defense of state authority be principled; it additionally insists that such a defense must rely on a particular kind of principle, namely one that draws no moral distinctions based on who is performing an action. This additional demand begs the question against the defender of state authority; it imposes on accounts of state authority a success condition that no defender of such authority would accept, and which guarantees from the outset that all defenses of such authority will fail.

To see how Anti-Exceptionalism stacks the deck against state authority, it will be useful to consider the case of parents. Mothers and fathers may treat their children in ways that no one else is permitted to treat them. A mother, for instance, may pick up her child and take her (nearly) anywhere in the world, even though, barring extenuating circumstances, no other adult may even touch the child. So, there is an action – picking up the child and taking her places – that only the child's parents may perform, in virtue of the fact that they are her parents. Now, "because they're her parents" is not really the bottom of the matter. One may reasonably ask why parents have this special authority, and many philosophers have done so.[11] But although justifications of parental authority must be principled, they do not need to show that parental rights are token instances of a type of right that anyone may hold. Parental rights, assuming they exist, are exceptional, one-of-a kind rights; no one but a particular parent can stand in the relationship to a particular child that generates such rights. Nevertheless, we must not infer from this lack of generality that defenses of parental rights are objectionably *ad hoc*. For such an inference would beg the question against the defender of parental rights; it would assume precisely what is at issue. To insist that a defender of parental rights must ground her defense in some feature of parents' situation that non-parents can share is simply to assume from the outset that there are no genuine parental rights.

---

11. For instance, Brighouse and Swift 2006; Gheaus 2012.

Anti-Exceptionalism begs the question against the defender of state authority in an analogous way. If there is genuine state authority, it will be one of a kind; it will rest on grounds distinct from those that support any other kind of authority, and it will exist only within citizen–state relationships. To insist on Anti-Exceptionalism is to stack the deck against state authority from the very beginning. In the next several sections, I will show how Huemer's remaining criticisms of my argument all turn on Anti-Exceptionalism and consequently fail.

4   Content Independence and Reasonable Disagreement

One of my aims in my first chapter was to show that legitimate states' right to rule – and citizens' corresponding obligation to obey – is content independent, at least to a considerable extent. This means that legitimate states have standing not just to publicize and enforce citizens' preexisting obligations but also to create a wide range of new obligations by passing laws. I argued that largely legitimate democracies – states that are merely flawed as opposed to failed – rule legitimately within the scope of their citizens' reasonable disagreement about their rights. My reasoning for this claim proceeded in two basic steps. First, for the state to serve its fundamental moral purpose of defining, adjudicating, and enforcing its citizens' rights within a structure of equal basic accountability, it must settle on particular laws with particular content; it must define, adjudicate, and enforce its citizens' rights in some particular ways rather than others. Second, citizens, to all of whom the state must stand in the same relationship of equal basic accountability, disagree reasonably and intractably about how the state should define, adjudicate, and enforce rights. Consequently, the laws of a reasonably legitimate democratic state are rightful, and command obedience, within the range of their citizens' reasonable disagreement about how it should carry out its proper function.

Huemer rejects my account of content independence on what I take to be three related grounds, and it will be best to consider them one by one. As we do, we will see that Anti-Exceptionalism plays an important role here, just as it does in his argument to the effect that I fail to respect rights as agent-centered constraints. Moreover, we will see that in implicitly appealing to Anti-Exceptionalism, Huemer again begs the question against the very idea of state authority, which must certainly be exceptional – though not necessarily unprincipled – if it exists at all.

Huemer's first line of attack against my account of content independence proceeds as follows. There is a strong moral presumption against coercion in the face of disagreement; when two people disagree, reasonably or not, we usually assume that both parties must refrain from coercing one another. But I have argued that reasonable disagreement among citizens on any matter within the state's purview is sufficient for the state's authority to pass and enforce democratically ratified law within the range of such disagreement. Since this violates the presumption against coercion in the face of reasonable disagreement, it must be wrong.

In offering this line of rebuttal, Huemer seems to be relying on the following background principle: If states have standing to coerce their citizens within the scope of their reasonable disagreements, then people in general must have standing to coerce one another whenever they reasonably disagree. This principle is just an application of Anti-Exceptionalism to the case of my argument about content-independence. And here again, Anti-Exceptionalism begs the question against my argument. I do not argue that states have standing to pass and enforce law within the scope of their citizens' reasonable disagreements because people, in general, have standing to coerce one another within the scope of reasonable disagreement. To the contrary, my argument is, as we have seen, highly specific to the context of the state-citizen relationship. Pointing out, as Huemer does, that there is a general presumption against coercion in the face of reasonable disagreement simply misses the point.

Huemer's second reply to my defense of content independence is, on the face of it, more promising than his first. I hold that states may pass and enforce a wide range of law and policy within the space of citizens' reasonable disagreement about the definition, adjudication, and enforcement of rights. But according to Huemer, much of actual law and policy bears no such relationship to rights. This is true, he argues, of one of my central examples: pharmaceutical regulation by the FDA. Concerning such regulation, I wrote that while some citizens might reasonably conclude that self-government is best served by low levels of pharmaceutical regulation, others might reasonably judge that

> since we must be able to rely on safe and effective medicine
> in order to plan our lives . . . as independent equals, the state

has standing to legislate, execute, and judge with respect to the quality and safety of drugs and keep those that fail off the market.[12]

In light of this reasonable disagreement, there is a wide range of legitimate FDA policy, including the current regime of testing and licensure. Huemer objects that the regulation and testing of drugs pertains to no rights whatsoever and so lacks a rational relationship to the state's proper function (according to me) of defining, adjudicating, and enforcing rights. He asks: "If the FDA didn't regulate drugs, how would that stop you from planning your life? Or from being independent? Or from having equal rights with everyone else?"[13] Let's take the three-component questions of Huemer's challenge in turn.

First, someone might reasonably suppose that we need drug regulation for life planning because, as embodied mortal beings, what we are able to do depends on the health of our bodies, and the health of our bodies depends on the quality and reliability of our access to medical care. If a major dimension of medical care is subject only to market forces, citizens – especially citizens who are not wealthy – will face constant uncertainty about the safety and efficacy of a major dimension of their care. Similar reasoning applies to independence; if citizens depend only on market forces for all dimensions of their pharmaceutical care, they depend on more powerful market actors within those dimensions. There are, of course, reasonable objections to these lines of argument, and I'm not at all sure that they should win the day. But that's okay for my position because what concerns me here is the scope of reasonable disagreement among citizens about rights-relevant matters, not how we should settle such disagreement in any particular case.

In asking how people might possibly lack equal rights without drug regulation, Huemer seems to be imagining that the rights in question are rights to publicly vetted drugs. It is, of course, true that if the state gives no one such a right, then it gives everyone the same (null) set of rights in this domain. But this doesn't entail that the absence of drug regulation wouldn't lead to rights-relevant

---

12. Layman, this book, Chapter 2, Section 6, p. 94.
13. Huemer, this book, Chapter 3, Section 4, p. 135.

inequalities elsewhere. For if we cannot depend on equally available pharmaceutical care, our ability to make equally effective use of our other rights may be limited by the interests and preferences of pharmaceutical companies and other powerful market actors. Once again, it does not strike me that this line of reasoning is conclusive. But it is manifestly reasonable, so it is admissible within the democratic process that must decide among competing reasonable points of view.

Huemer begins his third line of response to my account of content independence by granting (for the sake of argument) that there is some right or other (he imagines a right to "high-quality medical care," but the particular right isn't important) that the FDA's regulatory practices protect.[14] Even granting this much, he argues, there is no reason to think that the state may enforce the FDA's policies. He appeals to a version of the lifeboat scenario that he introduced in his first chapter:

> We're back on the lifeboat. You've just saved the lifeboat from sinking by forcing everyone to bail water. Now you notice a passenger who is sharing his potato chips with other passengers. You point out that potato chips are low-quality food, with too much saturated fat and acrylamide, but the passengers don't care; they go on eating. If it's reasonable to think there is a right to high quality health care, I suppose it is about equally reasonable to think there is a right to high quality food. Now, just as the FDA claims to improve the quality of medicine by prohibiting what it considers bad (unsafe, ineffective, or unproven) medicines, you on the lifeboat might try to improve the quality of food by prohibiting what you consider bad (unhealthful) foods. Since there could be reasonable disagreement about the right to high-quality food, does this mean it is permissible for you to forcibly seize the chips to prevent anyone from eating them?[15]

The answer, of course, is that it is not permissible forcibly to seize the chips. So, Huemer concludes, it is not permissible for the state

---

14. Huemer, this book, Chapter 3, Section 4, p. 135.
15. Huemer, this book, Chapter 3, Section 4, p. 135.

forcibly to prevent people from buying, selling, and using drugs that have not met its criteria. This move begs the question, and so misses the point, in exactly the same way that his first objection to my account of content-independence begs the question and misses the point. In appealing to his lifeboat example, Huemer assumes that if the state is justified in enforcing its pharmaceutical policies because those policies secure a right (to high-quality medicine), then anyone at all is justified in coercing anyone else whenever doing so stands to make it more likely that the coerced party will receive a benefit to which she has a right. Such a principle would, of course, be crazy. However, I am in no way committed to any such principle. An agent-neutral justification of this kind only appears relevant here if we assume the question-begging principle of Anti-Exceptionalism. My position about government's right to enforce the FDA's regulations turns on my account of why the state *is* exceptional, so arguments against it that depend on Anti-Exceptionalism simply fail to make contact with it.

5 Civil Disobedience and Respect

As we have seen, I argue that the authority of merely flawed (rather than failed) states is content independent within a fairly wide range, namely the range of reasonable disagreement among citizens about their rights. But this does not mean that citizens of such states are obligated to obey any law that their state might pass. Some laws can offend so deeply against the freedom and equality of some or all citizens that defenses of them are not just mistaken, but also unreasonable. When this is the case, citizens may, and sometimes even should, engage in civil disobedience. To disobey civilly, I explained, is not to ignore the law. Rather, a citizen disobeys civilly when she breaks a law openly, in a way that communicates both her judgment that it is too evil to be obeyed and the grounds of that judgment, and with the willingness to accept the legal consequences of her disobedience, including criminal punishment. Civil disobedience so understood, as opposed to mere conscientious refusal, is incumbent upon citizens who decide that they cannot in good conscience obey a law because only this form of disobedience respects the disobedient person's fellow citizens. Here again, as a reminder, is my explanation of why civilly disobedient citizens should not try to evade the legal consequences of their disobedience:

Civilly disobedient citizens should submit to legal proceedings for reasons similar to those that require civil disobedience to communicate clearly the content and grounds of the injustice that calls for disobedience. Assuming that my fellow citizens and I still share a legal framework that constitutes our equal freedom within our rights, my duty to respect them as equal rights-holders requires me to submit my judgment about the particular law that I have decided merits disobedience to the community's more basic legal norms and procedures. In particular, although civilly disobedient citizens can and should defend themselves vigorously in court, they should not attempt to evade either court proceedings or any penalties those proceedings might render. To do otherwise would be to treat one's own will and judgment as sovereign over others, and that would disrespect them and their equal rights.[16]

Huemer offers three lines of attack against my argument here. First, he argues that since we do not normally think that people have a duty to submit to unjust coercion, civilly disobedient citizens have no duty to accept punishment. Second, he argues that since no one has a right to pass or enforce unjust rules, only those who attempt to enforce such laws, and not those who evade punishment under them, disrespect rights. Third, he argues that even if, contrary to fact, evading punishment for violating unjust law did disrespect rights, it would be okay to evade the punishment anyway.

Huemer prosecutes the first of these arguments by relying on a version of his earlier lifeboat scenario:

Think about the lifeboat story again. Suppose that you've seized the potato chips from one of the passengers, declaring that no one may eat potato chips, due to your need to protect everyone from saturated fat. Several of the passengers on the boat think, correctly, that you are behaving very badly and have no right to seize anyone's chips. One of them also happens to have another bag of chips hidden in his coat. He is afraid of you, though, due to your penchant for waving your gun around and making

---

16. Layman, this book, Chapter 2, Section 8, p. 108. For an important recent account that differs in some respects from my own, see Delmas 2018.

irrational demands. So he takes the chips out surreptitiously and eats them in a corner of the boat while you aren't looking. You discover the passenger's disobedience when you find him holding an empty potato chip bag, with some potato crumbs on his shirt. You then demand that he submit to a beating, in punishment for his disobedience. . . . It is absurd to think that the passenger should submit to a beating. *You're* the one who acted reprehensibly in this story, so if anyone should be submitting to a beating, it should be you.[17]

You, of course, are meant to be analogous to the state here. Huemer reasons that if no one has a duty to accept a beating from you under these circumstances, then civilly disobedient citizens have no duty to submit to legal punishment.

Huemer's reasoning here again relies on Anti-Exceptionalism; if the potato chip enforcer on the boat has no standing to demand that anyone submit to a beating, then no state can have standing to demand that civilly disobedient citizens accept punishment. This line of thought ignores the possibility that there could be a special relationship between citizens and the state that does not exist between the potato chip enforcer and the other people on the boat, and which licenses the state to behave toward its citizens in a way that the enforcer may not behave toward her boatmates. Since my account of civil disobedience turns on just such a special relationship, the case of the potato chip enforcer makes no contact with it.

Huemer's second argument is more formidable. It takes seriously my claim that respect for our fellow citizens and their rights requires civilly disobedient citizens to accept their punishments, and it attempts to show that nobody holds any rights that one might respect by accepting the consequences of civil disobedience. Huemer writes that, for any given law meriting civil disobedience,

the government had no right to make the law in question in the first place, which is to say that the government had no right to issue threats of punishment for people who disobey that law . . . For the same reason, citizens who support that law had no right to have such a law passed or enforced; one cannot have a

---

17. Huemer, this book, Chapter 3, Section 5, p. 137.

right to have other people act unjustly and immorally. Therefore, evading enforcement of the law does not show disrespect
for anyone's rights; it is only the *enforcement* of the unjust law
that shows disrespect for rights.[18]

As I understand Huemer's argument in this passage, it proceeds
as follows:

1. If evading punishment for disobeying an unjust law disrespects
   a right, it disrespects a right to pass or enforce (or have passed
   or enforced by someone else) an unjust law.
2. There are no rights to pass or enforce (or have passed or
   enforced by someone else) an unjust law.
3. (From 2) Evading punishment for disobeying an unjust law
   does not disrespect a right to pass or enforce (or have passed or
   enforced by someone else) an unjust law.
4. Therefore, evading punishment for disobeying an unjust law
   does not disrespect a right.

I am happy to accept premise 2. However, I deny premise 1. For it
may be the case – and I have argued that it is the case – that civilly
disobedient citizens who evade the law disrespect, not some imagined right to pass or enforce unjust law, but rather the whole system
of rights whose definition, adjudication, and enforcement constitutes rule of law in their community. It is by respecting the rule of
law that we respect one another as equal rights-holders. Civil disobedience, as opposed to simple refusal to obey, only makes moral
sense to the extent that it is a response to a particular law within
a basically legitimate legal order – in our terminology, the legal
order of a merely flawed state as opposed to a failed one. Insofar as
we owe respect to one another as members of this system, we owe
it to one another to accept its verdicts, even when we reasonably
believe that a particular law is too evil to be obeyed. To do otherwise would be to treat our fellow citizens not as equally authoritative collaborators in a shared legal project, but instead as external
sources of sheer coercion.

---

18. Huemer, this book, Chapter 3, Section 5, p. 138.

Huemer's third reply to my account of civil disobedience proceeds by granting for the sake of argument that evading the consequences of civil disobedience does disrespect one's fellow citizens. Even if we assume that such evasion is thus disrespectful, he contends, it is still okay for civilly disobedient citizens to evade punishment. This is because it is okay to insult people in order to avoid suffering terrible consequences that others might unrightfully inflict on you. Huemer writes:

> Suppose you go up to a neighbor and say, "You disgust me. I have no respect at all for you or your supposed 'rights'. You are inferior to me and fit only to serve me." Then you turn your back and walk away. In doing this, you would be expressing disrespect for the neighbor and his equal rights, *far* more clearly than you would by merely evading punishment for breaking a law. And, in normal circumstances, that would certainly be a bad thing to do. But let's add to the story. Imagine that the *reason* you did this was that there is a group of terrorists who were going to kidnap you and hold you hostage for five years in dangerous, unsanitary, and terrifying conditions. The police can't stop them. You can't defend yourself from them. You can't run or hide from them. The *only* way you could avoid being taken prisoner by the terrorists was to give them what they want. And the only thing they want is for you to viciously insult your neighbor, as described above. (Just accept this odd scenario for the sake of argument.) *Now* what do we think about your action? It doesn't seem so bad anymore.[19]

Huemer assumes here that when I say that evading the consequences of civil disobedience disrespects one's fellow citizens, I mean that such evasion insults them, or expresses to them a message with the content, "I don't respect you!" But this is not what I mean at all. Disrespecting people in the sense that is relevant here is not the same thing as insulting them. Rather, to disrespect someone is to treat her as lacking a particular kind of value or standing that she in fact possesses.[20]

---

19. Huemer, this book, Chapter 3, Section 5, pp. 138–139.
20. Interestingly, Huemer's misinterpretation of disrespectful civic behavior as insulting civic behavior is almost identical to Jason Brennan and Peter Jaworski's misinterpretation of disrespectful market behavior as insulting market behavior. See Brennan and Jaworski 2015, Chapter 5.

An example might help to clarify what I mean. Suppose that you are a manager at a firm and that your employees submit weekly reports with suggestions for how their assigned projects could proceed more successfully. All of your employees dutifully submit their reports each week, but you never do more than glance at the reports written by women. This disrespects them; it constitutes a failure to respond appropriately to the value and standing they, in fact, possess. However, it does not necessarily insult them, since, under normal circumstances, your behavior doesn't communicate any message to anyone. To be sure, the women who work for you would likely be insulted if they found out about your behavior. But that is not why your behavior is wrong. To the contrary, it is wrong because it is disrespectful, and it is in virtue of its being disrespectful that the women would be insulted if they found out about it.

Evading the consequences of civil disobedience is likewise disrespectful because it fails to recognize and respond to a kind of standing that certain other people possess, not because it is insulting to anyone. In particular, it fails to recognize and respond to the equal standing that one's fellow citizens have to decide on how the law should define, adjudicate, and enforce rights within a shared, mutually accountable system of law. All citizens have, in virtue of their shared relationship within this system, standing to insist that their fellow citizens submit their grievances with the law, however reasonable they might be, to the processes of legal adjudication through which each citizen may make her case to the rest. Evading the consequences of civil disobedience disrespects this standing, and that is why it is wrong. Whether anyone is insulted is simply not to the point.

6   Summary

I have responded to Huemer's critique of my first chapter by defending four primary positions.

First, I argued that power is nonarbitrary to the extent that it is accountable, not to the extent that it is impossible for a powerful person to interfere. States can secure their citizens' rights against such power to a considerable, albeit imperfect, extent by defining, adjudicating, and enforcing their citizens' rights within legal institutions subject to equal basic democratic accountability.

Second, I showed how my claim that the state may coerce us for the sake of our rights is not in tension with the idea, which I accept, that rights are agent-centered constraints. Since suitably structured states have a right to rule, no one has a right not to be ruled by his or her suitably structured state, which, in turn, means that the state need not violate any agent-centered constraints in order to rule.

Third, I made explicit Huemer's implicit methodological assumption of Anti-Exceptionalism, according to which states are justified in doing something just in case anyone at all would be justified in doing the same (narrowly described) thing under the same (narrowly described) circumstances. This assumption, I argued, begs the question against my position, which turns on an account of why the state is exceptional in a way that justifies its agents in doing things that no one else could be justified in doing.

Fourth and fifth, I drew on the earlier sections of this chapter to answer Huemer's challenges to my accounts of content independence and civil disobedience, respectively. Concerning content independence, I argued that citizens are obligated to obey the law of at least reasonably democratically accountable states to the extent that its content falls within the scope of citizens' reasonable disagreement about their rights. This is not because of any general principle that says that coercion is okay whenever there is reasonable disagreement about rights, but rather because the state must, for the sake of all citizens' liberty within their rights, define, adjudicate, and enforce rights in the face of reasonable disagreement among citizens about how it should do so. Similarly, I argued that civilly disobedient citizens should accept the consequences of their disobedience, not because people should generally accept unjust coercion, but because democratic citizens are obligated to respect one another by respecting the rule of law that constitutes the conditions of their equal freedom within rights.

Bibliography

Brennan, Jason and Peter Jaworski. 2015. *Markets Without Limits: Moral Virtues and Commercial Interests*. New York: Routledge.

Brighouse, Harry and Adam Swift. 2006. "Parents' Rights and the Value of the Family", *Ethics* 117 (1): 80–108.

Delmas, Candice. 2018. *A Duty to Resist: When Disobedience Should be Uncivil*. New York: Oxford University Press.

Dworkin, Ronald. 1986. *Law's Empire*. Cambridge, MA: Belknap.

Gaus, Gerald. 2003. "Backwards Into the Future: Neo-Republicanism as a Post-Socialist Critique of Market Society", *Social Philosophy & Policy* 20 (1): 59–91.

Gheaus, Anca. 2012. "The Right to Parent One's Biological Baby", *Journal of Political Philosophy* 20 (4): 432–455.

Pettit, Philip. 1997. *Republicanism: A Theory of Freedom and Government*. New York: Oxford University Press.

Warren v. District of Columbia, 444 A.2d 1.

Second Round of Replies

Chapter 5

A Second Reply to Layman on Authority

Michael Huemer

Contents

I'd like to thank Daniel Layman for another interesting reply, and also for participating in this debate in general. I'm afraid I didn't understand everything in his last reply, though, which may make it difficult to respond, but I'll do my best anyway. I also don't have space to discuss everything that came up. In particular, I'm not going to discuss how well capitalism or anarcho-capitalism works. I disagree with everything Layman says about that, and I see no hope of making progress on that without writing a whole other book.[1] I'm not going to further discuss the FDA either, but I will recommend another book on that in the footnotes.[2]

In the interest of making some progress, I'd like to focus on just a few issues. I'm going to discuss (1) the accountability of government,

---

1. See part 2 of my *The Problem of Political Authority* and David Friedman's *The Machinery of Freedom*.
2. See Jessica Flanigan, *Pharmaceutical Freedom: Why Patients Have a Right to Self-Medicate* (New York: Oxford University Press, 2017).

DOI: 10.4324/9780429328046-9

(2) the nature of rights as constraints, (3) the "Anti-Exceptionalism" principle, and (4) civil disobedience.

I   Is Government Accountable?

Let's start with accountability. The government, we agree, *should* be accountable to citizens for protecting them, respecting their rights, and generally doing its job. By my lights, however, government is clearly not, in fact, accountable for these things. Here is how Layman defined "accountability":

> A is accountable to . . . B to the extent that (1) A owes something to B; (2) B has standing to insist to A that A discharge her obligation; and (3) B can rely on institutional backup in support of her claim against A.
>
> (Chapter 2, Section 5)

So for the government to be accountable to you, it must be the case that you can *insist* that the government fulfill its obligations to you, and you can rely on *institutional backup* in support of this insistence. But that's clearly false. As Layman has acknowledged, if you try to sue the government for not fulfilling its obligations to you (e.g., for not protecting you), your suit will be summarily dismissed. Now, I am not assuming that tort liability is *the only possible* way that the government could be accountable. That was just an illustration of the general fact that *there is nothing you can do* to *hold* the government accountable. You also can't, for example, initiate criminal prosecution against the government. Nor can you effectively complain to some other tribunal (you could try complaining to the United Nations, but this, of course, will go nowhere). And there just simply isn't any other relevant institution out there that you can appeal to. So condition (3) is false; you cannot count on institutional backup in support of your claim against the government. So there's no accountability, on Layman's own definition.

Perhaps Layman would say there is some *other* institutional backup for your claim against the government. What might this be? All he says is that there is "democratic accountability," which is "the equal basic accountability of a political community's whole system of law and policy to its democratically represented people." Unfortunately, I don't know what this means. It reads to me like a phrase that simply *assumes* that democratic governments are accountable but doesn't attempt to explain how that's so. If the government has not fulfilled its obligations to you, *what exactly* can you do about it? And exactly what institution is going to support you, in what way?

My only guess is that Layman would say, "You can vote against the incumbent politicians, and the democratic system will support you by expelling the politicians from office, provided that a majority of voters agree with you." But this is an extremely poor mechanism of accountability. It has approximately zero chance of success, and the existence of this mechanism provides little meaningful constraint on politicians, for reasons explained in my previous reply which I will not repeat here.

Take a concrete case of government failure, say, the case of *Warren v. District of Columbia*, discussed in my previous reply (Chapter 3, Section 2.3): you've just been beaten, robbed, and raped because the police culpably failed to protect you after your two calls for help. Presumably, they violated their duties to you. What exactly does Layman imagine that you could do about this, and what institutional backup could you count on receiving?

Imagine Layman answering: "You can vote against the mayor in the next election." Does this really establish a meaningful form of accountability? I don't think so. First, the odds of your actually causing the mayor to be removed from office are, in normal cases, approximately zero. Second, even if the mayor is removed from office, the police officers who failed to protect you will almost certainly not be fired, nor suffer any other penalty whatsoever. You definitely won't get any compensation for your suffering, either.

In introducing the notion of accountability to begin with, Layman gave an example involving students' rights to equal treatment, fair grading, etc. (Chapter 2, Section 5). Let's think about that again. Imagine that at your university, students have frequent complaints about unfair grading. By university policy, all grade complaints are summarily dismissed, regardless of the merits. However, there is a rule that, if you can obtain one million handwritten signatures on a petition, you can get the dean of the college fired from his job. This would not result in your grade being changed, nor would your actual professor be punished in any way. Now, would that convince you that all professors were "accountable to you for fair grading"?

That is analogous to the claim that the government is accountable because you can try to get politicians voted out of office.

Maybe my focus has been too individualistic. Maybe Layman would agree that the government is not accountable to you specifically, but he would claim that it is accountable to *society as a whole*. I have doubts about this, as I don't think "society" names an agent, and I don't think it makes sense to say someone is accountable to something that isn't an agent. But even if this made sense, I don't think it would establish what the defender of authority wants. The defender of authority does not only want to say that "society" has obligations to the government. The defender of authority wants to say that *you specifically* have an obligation of obedience to the government. I don't see how that obligation would be established by the government's being accountable to something or someone else, not to you.

Layman could just *stipulate* that the ability of a majority of citizens to vote political leaders out of office counts as a form of "accountability": "democratic accountability." But then the question would remain: Who cares about this democratic accountability? What would that have to do with my being obligated to obey anyone or with anyone's having a right to rule over me?

Return to my Democratic Dinner Party example (Chapter 1, Section 4.2): After going out to dinner with four other people, three of the others tell me they want me to pay for everyone. Do they have the right to force me to pay? Do I have an obligation to pay? The answer is obviously "no" to both questions. Now suppose we make the following modifications: Suppose the three people *first* vote that Bob should dictate the distribution of the bill (they do this knowing that Bob will put the entire bill on me). Then Bob declares that I have to pay for everyone's meal. *Now* do I have to pay for everyone? Before you answer, note that Bob is now "accountable" in the sense that three people could vote for someone else to be the bill distributor instead of him (he's still not accountable *to me* though).

I don't see how this makes any difference at all. Maybe if *I* had chosen Bob, then I'd have some kind of obligation to follow his directions. But not if some other people just chose him because they wanted him to impose their will on me. Putting the label "democratic accountability" on such a situation may make it sound nicer, but it does nothing to explain why my usual rights would be suspended.

2   Rights as Side Constraints

Coercing other people is typically wrong and a violation of their rights. I want to know why the government is entitled to coerce people in all sorts of circumstances in which no one else would be entitled to do so. Part of Layman's answer was something like this: "Because government is needed to prevent other people from committing even more coercion." That answer seems to me to ignore the nature of rights as *agent-centered constraints*: It assumes that it's okay to violate someone's rights as long as you prevent a larger number of rights-violations.

Now, here is Layman's reply, as far as I understand it (Chapter 4, Section 2): He *agrees* that rights function as constraints, so you can't violate a right even to prevent more rights-violations by others. But he claims that we never had a right not to be coerced *by a democratic government*. We only had a right to not be coerced by nongovernment agents and undemocratic governments. As he says, the right against coercion is *conditional* – you have a right not to be coerced *if* certain conditions obtain.

Now, I'm not disagreeing that there can be conditional rights, or that exceptions can be built into a right. But not just *anything* can be one of the conditions for a right to apply. I'm not saying that *merely* attaching conditions to a right automatically means that you're rejecting the idea of agent-centered constraints. I am saying that *some* conditions that you could attach would amount to rejecting the notion of rights as agent-centered constraints.

Background: Utilitarianism and Consequentialism

In ethics, the arch-opponents of agent-centered constraints are the *consequentialists*. Consequentialism is the view that the right action is always the action that produces the best total consequences. Utilitarianism is a form of consequentialism that says that the good is happiness or desire-satisfaction; hence, the right action is always the action that maximizes the total quantity of happiness or desire-satisfaction in the world.

Example: Say there's a philosopher known as Al the Utilitarian. Al thinks that it's okay to kill an innocent person to prevent two innocent people from being killed. Layman and I would, I presume, object that this is not okay because there is a right to life, and you can't violate a right even to prevent two comparable rights-violations by someone else. Now imagine Al responding to this: "Oh no, you're getting confused. My view is perfectly compatible with the right to life being an agent-centered constraint. It's just that the right is *conditional.* You have a right not to be killed *unless* killing you is necessary to prevent more killings. So killing one person to save two is perfectly okay, even though rights are agent-centered constraints."

That response by Al must be wrong since it would defeat the point of speaking of agent-centered constraints – if we accept Al's response, then *any* view (even utilitarianism) could count as "endorsing agent-centered constraints." To be meaningful, the notion of moral constraints has to exclude *certain kinds* of conditions. In particular, a moral constraint cannot contain a clause whereby the constraint doesn't apply provided that a greater good is to be produced, or greater harm avoided, or a greater number of violations of the constraint avoided.

With that understood, it cannot be that our right against coercion contains an exception clause whereby the right doesn't apply if coercing us would prevent more coercion by someone else. Now, Layman didn't *exactly* propose that exception (he didn't say exactly what condition he was proposing). But the exception that his view requires is *uncomfortably close* to that. There would have to be an exception built into our right against coercion whereby the right doesn't apply against the government if the government's coercing us is necessary to prevent a larger total amount of coercion. That may not be *formally inconsistent* with the notion of an agent-centered constraint, but it's completely implausible if you believe in agent-centered constraints.

Now, one of the widely accepted exceptions to rights is the "defense" exception: An action that would normally be a violation of X's rights becomes okay (and not a rights-violation) if it is necessary to defend against rights-violating behavior *by X himself.* For example, if someone is about to commit a murder, you can kill him to stop him from doing it. But note that it's essential that the person whom you are coercing is also the source of the threat that you're defending against. If you remove that element, and you say "It's okay to coerce X to prevent *other people* from committing more coercion," then you've abandoned a rights theory for a consequentialist theory, in substance if not in name.

3 Anti-Exceptionalism

Layman thinks that I endorse a principle called "Anti-Exceptionalism":

> Condition C justifies action A when performed by the state if, and only if, C justifies A when performed by anyone at all.

He also thinks that this principle "begs the question against the defender of state authority" and "imposes on accounts of state authority a success condition that no defender of such authority would accept, and which guarantees from the outset that all defenses of such authority will fail" (Chapter 4, Section 3).

I'm not sure I understand Anti-Exceptionalism, so I don't know whether I endorse it. I know that I didn't beg any questions, though, nor did I lay down any principle that rules out defenses of authority at the start. So let me just start with the principle I actually endorse. I endorse what is called *the supervenience of moral properties* ("Supervenience" for short):

> **Supervenience:** There cannot be a moral difference between two things without some descriptive difference between them that explains the moral difference.

For example, it cannot be that John and Jack are identical in *all* relevant respects (they have exactly the same character traits, beliefs, desires, intentions, and *all other* relevant characteristics), but John is good and Jack evil. That just doesn't make sense. Similarly, it cannot be that action A and action B have exactly the same characteristics, except that A is morally right and B morally wrong. If one is right and the other wrong, there has to be some other way in which they differ that explains why one is right and the other wrong.

This is not a controversial principle; it's trivial. To see why, let me explain why one sort of objection fails. You might think: "I have a counter-example. Plato back in ancient Greece owned slaves, and he *wasn't* a horrible person. But anyone who owned slaves in our society today would be a horrible person, even if the modern-day person treated his slaves in exactly the same way Plato treated his." (Note: I'm not interested in arguing about whether Plato was really horrible. Just assume the views in quotes for the sake of argument.)

Now, that is *not* a counter-example to Supervenience. We could ask, "Okay, why is it that Plato wasn't horrible, but a slave-owner today would be?," and there *would be an answer*. It doesn't matter *what* the answer is, as long as it cites some descriptive difference. For instance, suppose you think slave-owning by Plato was not so bad because Plato, unlike us, grew up in a culture where he was taught that slave-owning was okay, he saw people all around him doing it, etc. Well, that explanation cites *descriptive differences* between Plato and a modern-day slave-holder, or between Plato's action and that of the modern person. So that is perfectly consistent with the Supervenience principle. The principle does not place any restrictions on what the descriptive difference between the cases could be; it does not, for example, rule out that features of Plato's *society* could be relevant to our moral evaluation of him. The only things that would violate Supervenience would be (a) if there was no reason whatsoever why Plato's slave-owning would be less bad than modern-day slave-owning, and yet it was still less bad, or (b) the only reasons that could be given were other evaluative differences, which could not themselves be explained by any descriptive differences (e.g., "it was less bad because it was less immoral," where no one could explain what made it less immoral).

So, I accept the Supervenience principle, *as do all ethicists*. And I implicitly applied it in my opening statement when I described the case of the vigilante who imposes his rules on his neighborhood and extorts payment from his neighbors (Chapter 1, Section 1.1). If the vigilante's behavior is wrong and the government's is right, I have assumed, then there must be *some reason* why this is so.

Now suppose someone tries to explain why the government's behavior is okay. Suppose the theory is "Because the government satisfies condition C, and the vigilante does not." Then an implication of this theory is that *if* the vigilante *did* satisfy C, then his behavior would also be okay. So it's fair game to describe, if possible, a modification to the case whereby the vigilante satisfies C, and then solicit people's intuitions as to whether he'd then be entitled to extort and impose his will on his neighbors. (Notice that I'm not *assuming* that it *is* possible to describe such a case. I'm saying that *if* there is such a case, it's relevant to consider.)

I think this is what Layman is objecting to. But this really does not involve any controversial assumption either. If C is really the complete reason why the government's behavior is okay, then *by definition*, if the vigilante satisfies C, his behavior will be okay.

If *the relevant difference* between the vigilante and the state was just that the state satisfies C but the vigilante doesn't, then if we make the vigilante satisfy C (while changing nothing else relevant about the case), then the vigilante and the government will be alike in all relevant respects. By Supervenience, their actions must then have the same moral status.

Let's illustrate this with a particular theory of authority. The most famous theory of political authority is the Social Contract Theory (see Chapter 1, Section 2): *The state has authority because we made an agreement to grant it authority.* That's a legitimate example of a theory of authority if anything is. Does this theory respect Supervenience? Of course it does. The relevant difference between the state and the vigilante is, allegedly, that we made a social contract with the state, and we didn't make any similar contract with any vigilantes. Now, it's an implication of this theory that *if* we made a contract with a vigilante whereby we all agreed to have him round up vandals and we also agreed that he could demand money from us and force us to pay, then we *would* be obligated to pay the vigilante, and he *would* be entitled to round up vandals and force us to pay. And that, as a matter of fact, is perfectly fine. Social contract theorists would have no problem with any of this. So the Supervenience principle certainly does not beg the question against defenders of authority, nor does the principle rule out political authority at the start, nor would defenders of authority, in general, reject it. (In fact, I don't think anyone other than possibly Daniel Layman rejects Supervenience.)

Of course, the social contract theory fails because it's factually false: We did not, in fact, sign any social contract. That's what rules the theory out, not the Supervenience principle. Now, maybe there are *other* theories that *are* ruled out by the Supervenience principle. But that doesn't show that Supervenience begs any questions. Any argument against P – where P is any philosophical position – is going to have premises that (jointly) conflict with P – that's just what it means to have an argument "against P." And there are always going to be P-believers who reject different premises of the argument. That doesn't make those premises question-begging or in any other way defective. And in this particular case, again, Supervenience is just about the least controversial idea in ethics, so it's completely reasonable to assume it, and completely unreasonable to deny it simply to maintain a doctrine of authority.

Here is an analogy to explain how I see the exchange between Layman and myself. Let's say there are two people, Don and Mark, who are interested in the relative merits of different fruits:

Don: Oranges are the only good fruit.

Mark: What makes them so good?

Don: They are sweet.

Mark: But grapes are just as sweet. So the sweetness of oranges couldn't make them better than grapes.

Don: You're begging the question by assuming that oranges aren't *exceptional*. My theory is just that oranges are exceptional, in that they can be made good by features that wouldn't make other fruits good. In particular, the sweetness of oranges makes them good, but it doesn't make grapes good.

Mark: Why are oranges exceptional?

Don: Because they are sweet.

In this exchange, Don is confused. Mark didn't beg any questions, and Don's theory makes no sense. It cannot be that the sweetness of oranges makes them better than something else that's equally sweet. Nor can the sweetness of oranges give them the ability to be made better by that very sweetness than other, equally sweet fruits.

That's like my exchange with Daniel Layman. He says it's okay for the government to coerce us in various ways that (we both agree) it's *not* okay for private individuals or organizations to do. I ask why the government is so special. He says the government is special because it has some feature – say, because it's democratic. I say, "Well, here's an example of someone who has that feature, and you agree that this person is *not* entitled to coerce people. [See, e.g., the Democratic Dinner Party example here.] So that feature can't explain why the government is entitled to coerce us." Layman then accuses me of begging the question by assuming that the government isn't exceptional. As best I can guess, what makes the government exceptional is supposed to be the very same feature(s) already cited (e.g., that it's democratic).

Layman seems to be claiming that the relevant difference between the government and private agents can be something that isn't even a difference between them – that is, one can cite a feature that the government actually shares with some private agents, yet claim that it explains why the government gets to do things that those private agents don't get to do. This is like the theory that the reason why oranges are better than *equally sweet* grapes is that oranges are sweet.

The only way I can think of to make the view coherent is to suppose that Layman is actually claiming that the property of "being a government" is just *intrinsically* morally significant. That is, the complete reason the government is entitled to coerce us isn't really that they have this property of "democratic accountability"; the real, complete reason they're entitled to coerce us is that they have democratic accountability *plus* the property of being a government. Furthermore, there is no explanation of why "being a government" is morally significant – that's just a brute moral fact.

If *that's* the theory, then of course I can't raise a counterexample involving a private agent who has that feature. When the theory appealed *merely* to democratic accountability, I could raise examples of agents who have democratic accountability but aren't entitled to coerce anyone. But by definition, I can't raise an example of a private agent with the feature of "being a government."

However, this is an extremely implausible theory, in the same way that the theory that "being an orange" is intrinsically morally significant is implausible. If Layman was going to say something like this, he might as well have foregone all the complicated discussion about democratic accountability, remedying the defects of the state of nature, and so on. If you're willing to claim that "being a government" is just fundamentally, *intrinsically* morally significant, then you might as well just say, "My theory is that democratic governments have authority in virtue of the property of *being democratic governments*." In fine, "It's just a brute fact that democratic governments are entitled to rule over us." That would be much simpler, and just as plausible.

By the way, it's worth thinking about who is actually begging the question here. I did not lay down a condition that no theory of authority could satisfy. Layman, however, has advanced an unfalsifiable theory. If you just start out saying that governments have authority partly in virtue of *being governments*, and you declare this as a brute, inexplicable fact, then of course no one could refute this.

Now, I suspect that Layman is going to deny that he did that. I suspect he'll claim that he *gave a theory* of why the government is "exceptional." But he didn't – at least, not a coherent, noncircular one. He might say, "My theory of why government is exceptional is this: because they have democratic accountability, etc." But no, that's not an explanation of why they are *exceptional*. Being "exceptional" in this context, by definition, means that you have special rights or privileges that *do not* accrue to other agents who have democratic accountability, etc. To explain that, one would have to cite something other than democratic accountability, etc.

I suspect that Layman got caught in some circular thinking, something like the following: "Government has authority because it has feature F. Mike objects that other agents with F don't have authority. Ah, but that's okay because feature F is enough to confer authority *if you're the government* but not if you're a private agent. Why? Well, governments are different from private agents, because they have authority."

4   Civil Disobedience

I have space to discuss one more issue: Should people who rightly violate unjust laws also willingly submit to punishment from the government? Layman (Chapter 4, Section 5) says yes; I find the idea absurd.

One of my arguments was that the government has no right to pass or enforce an unjust law, nor does any citizen have a right to have unjust laws enforced. In his recent reply, Layman agrees with this; however, he claims that failure to accept punishment shows disrespect for "the whole system of rights whose definition, adjudication, and enforcement constitutes rule of law in [one's] community."

Unfortunately, I don't understand how that's supposed to be true. Let's say I respect all genuine rights, I follow all just laws, I only violate unjust laws, and I try to avoid punishment for violating unjust laws. I can see how this might be thought to show disrespect *for the unjust laws*. I have no idea how it would also show disrespect for the *just* laws, or for anyone's actual rights. What rights, exactly, am I disrespecting, and how? Surely one has to give some more specific answer than "the whole system."

Maybe the claim is that one disrespects "the rule of law" by violating a law. Now I don't know why there would be anything wrong with disrespecting the rule of law. What is the rule of law anyway? Maybe it's the principle that laws should always be followed (*including* unjust ones)? Or that they should always be enforced? Or at least that's *part* of it? If so, then obviously I reject the rule of law, and I think no one should respect such a false principle.

But anyway, if you think there's some sort of obligation to respect the rule of law, then *the original disobedience* must be wrong. So how could Layman claim that you're justified in disobeying an unjust law yet *not* justified in avoiding punishment? How would the avoidance of punishment disrespect the rule of law any more than *breaking the law* disrespects the rule of law?

I can't understand Layman's view there. Nevertheless, let's move on to a final point. In my previous reply, I argued that disrespect is only a minor sin anyway, easily outweighed by the importance of avoiding severe, unjust harm like being unjustly imprisoned for multiple years. To support this, I gave an example in which you are justified in viciously insulting your neighbor because doing so is necessary to prevent you from being kidnapped and held captive by terrorists for 5 years.

Layman's response is to say that I misunderstood the notion of "disrespect" – I mistakenly thought disrespect was merely *insulting* someone. He cites an example in which a manager makes employees write reports but he never reads the reports written by women. He never *tells* anyone that he's doing this, so no one is insulted; still, he is disrespecting the women. That shows that you can have disrespect without insult.

Fair enough. But that doesn't dispute my argument. My argument did not require that insulting someone be *the only possible way* of disrespecting someone. It only required that insulting someone be *a way* of disrespecting them. As long as that's true, my example succeeds in showing that the badness of disrespect is outweighed by the importance of avoiding unjust punishment.

The same point could be made using Layman's example of the company manager disrespecting female employees. That behavior certainly sounds bad initially. But now let me add this to the story: Suppose that the reason why this manager never reads reports written by women is that if he were ever to read a report written by a woman, a bizarre terrorist group would kidnap him and hold him prisoner for 5 years in a dungeon. In that case, he is completely justified in not reading those reports, no matter how disrespectful this may be.

Now, maybe you could argue that in that case, his refusal to read the reports isn't disrespectful anymore. That isn't really the point, though. *Even if* it's disrespectful, it would be crazy to think that means the manager has to let the terrorists kidnap him. The general point, again, is that *the badness of disrespect is outweighed by the importance of avoiding serious, unjust, tangible harm.* Indeed, next to a harm like being imprisoned for 5 years, the putative evil of mere disrespect (disrespect that doesn't have any further negative consequences) pales into insignificance.

Therefore, even if evading punishment is somehow disrespectful to other people, that consideration is insignificant in comparison with the importance of avoiding yourself being sent to prison. I would, in fact, be happy to be disrespected all day if that would prevent someone else from being unjustly imprisoned. Every decent person should feel the same way.

5   Conclusion

In his original chapter, I thought that Layman's defense of political authority was something like this: The government has authority because

a)   It is needed to protect our rights (and is reasonably good at doing so).
b)   It is accountable to all of us.

I thought that the operative notion of accountability was one implying that an individual citizen actually has some feasible *recourse* if the government fails in its duties, some reasonably likely means of attaining some kind of remedy.

Now, however, it appears to me that Layman is advancing a more stipulative and question-begging defense of authority. Layman's notion of "accountability," as far as I understand it, does not actually require there to be any practicable recourse available to individual citizens; rather, we just stipulate that the government counts as "accountable" if it's democratic.

I think the most important objection is that conditions (a) and (b) don't explain authority because you can imagine people or organizations with those features yet without authority. For example, you can imagine a group of people voting to appoint someone to violate other people's rights. The violator will count as "accountable" in the stipulative democratic sense, but that wouldn't make his actions cease to be rights violations. You can also imagine someone effectively protecting other people's rights and preventing various bad things from happening, yet this wouldn't give that agent a right to *also* forcibly impose plans that are *not* necessary to protecting rights (as the government regularly does). So, if government has authority, it can't be just because it has features (a) and (b).

As far as I now understand Layman's position, he holds that (a) and (b) confer authority on the government, but they wouldn't confer authority on anyone else who had those features. This is because government is "exceptional," in the sense that it can be justified in doing things for reasons that wouldn't justify similar behavior by anyone else. And the reason the government is exceptional is . . . that it has features (a) and (b).

This theory makes no sense. It is like the theory that the sweetness of oranges makes them better than other fruits that are equally sweet. Alternately, Layman's position may be that the real source of government's authority is not merely (a) and (b); rather, the full theory is that the government has authority because

a) It is needed to protect our rights (and is reasonably good at doing so);
b) It is accountable to all of us; and
c) It is a government.

Including condition (c) amounts to simply assuming that government is inherently special and refusing to give any reason why.

I don't really blame Layman, though. It's not his fault. It's due to the position he was tasked with defending. The belief in government authority is a prejudice, inculcated into us by our culture and by the government itself, that has no actual rational basis. When you try to defend such a prejudice, it's very common that you fall into circular arguments, assuming the key point in dispute without explanation, rejecting principles that are uncontroversial in other contexts, and rejecting whole genres of argument as applied to your thesis (as Layman rejects analogical arguments). That's just what we should expect given the nonexistence of authority.

Chapter 6

A Second Reply to Huemer on Authority

Daniel Layman

Contents

Once again, I would like to begin by thanking Michael Huemer for contributing the remarks to which I will respond. This final chapter will reply to his concerns one by one before offering some brief closing remarks.

I Accountability

In the first section of the previous chapter, Huemer continues to insist that governments cannot be accountable in any sense that might ground their authority. This, he says, is because individuals usually cannot force government agents to do things apart from the political process. I granted earlier that citizens generally cannot force state agents to do things apart from the political process. However, I denied that this necessarily undercuts the accountability necessary for democratic authority, because governments can be – and, to a considerable extent, sometimes are – accountable to the political community through the democratic process. Moreover, I pointed out that the degree to which individual citizens should be able to force state agents to do things is itself a subject of ongoing

DOI: 10.4324/9780429328046-10

dispute among citizens and, consequently, answerable to judgments issued through the democratic process. In response, Huemer says that since individual citizens can't make government agents do what they want, governments are unaccountable to citizens, even in the best democracies. So, governments are not accountable in the way that my account needs for them to be.

The answer to this attack is very simple, and in case it was unclear before, I'll make it extremely explicit now: Accountability of the kind that matters to democratic authority is always, in the first place, accountability to the whole political community of equal citizens. This means that while governments are accountable to individuals for applying the laws evenly, no individual citizen has standing to insist that government agents treat her in ways other than those established by law, which, in turn, means that it is not a problem for views like mine that individual people are rarely able to make agents of the state do what they want. Insofar as I am an equal member of a democratic political community, I share in the accountability that exists between the political community and its government. But I do not have moral standing to sidestep the political community's processes and make the government enact what I take to be justice in my own cases. If I did have such standing, I would have standing to insist that my private judgment dictate the action of the ostensibly public government, whose moral standing turns on its equal relationship to all its citizens.

Interpreting democratic accountability as accountability that is, in the first place, accountability to political communities does not require me to abandon my stated conception of accountability. That conception, Huemer reminds us, goes like this:

> A is accountable to . . . B to the extent that (1) A owes something to B; (2) B has standing to insist to A that A discharge her obligation; and (3) B can rely on institutional backup in support of her claim against A.

Let me spell out how this notion of accountability works in the cases of government accountability to the body politic and government accountability to individuals, respectively.

First, government is accountable to the political community insofar as (1) government owes definition, enforcement, and adjudication of rights to the political community in accordance with its democratic judgments; (2) the political community has standing to insist that the government define, enforce, and adjudicate rights in accordance with its democratic judgments; and (3) the political community can rely on backup if some agent of the government refuses to comply with its democratic judgments. For example, suppose, in keeping with our discussion on this topic so far, that a democratic political community duly deliberates and decides to limit prosecutors' civil (or criminal) liability under a wide range of circumstances. In this case, relevant government agents owe it to the political community to act on this judgment, and the community has standing to insist that those agents do so. Moreover, if accountability is duly in place, the community will be able to rely on enforcement if renegade state actors attempt to facilitate forbidden litigation or prosecution against the protected parties. If such accountability is not duly in place, renegade actors may be able to get away with facilitating such litigation or prosecution in violation of the political community's decision. Once again, I want to emphasize that I am not endorsing immunity for prosecutors on its merits; quite the contrary. I am simply pointing out how government can be properly accountable to the whole democratic political community for carrying out its legal decision to grant such immunity.

Second, government is accountable to each individual as a member of the political community insofar as (1) government owes equal application of the laws to each individual; (2) each individual has standing to insist on equal application in her case; and (3) each individual can rely on backup if some agent of the government denies her equal application. So, to stick with our example, if the community decides to limit liability for prosecutors, it owes evenhanded application of this legal decision to each of its citizens, and each citizen must, in a legitimate state, be able to count on support if state agents fail to deliver evenhanded application. If, for instance, the law against liability for prosecutors is applied in practice to non-white citizens hoping to take those officials to court but not to white citizens, this would seriously undermine democratic accountability on the individual level, thus damaging political legitimacy in that community. But if the political community determines – again, in my judgment, wrongly – that low levels of liability for prosecutors is the best policy and then enforces that policy across the board, this does not necessarily amount to a diminution of government accountability in the sense relevant to authority.

2 Rights

I argued in my previous chapter that rights are usually conditional, and that although agents of the state, like all other people, do not have standing to demand money from you or handcuff you simply to pursue their own desires or projects, they may have the right to do so in the course of enforcing appropriately democratically accountable law. You and I do typically have a right against being handcuffed and so forth, but that right is, like all of our rights, conditional on the handcuffing party lacking a special right to handcuff us. An account of how state agents may, under the right circumstances, do such things as handcuff people is, of course, nothing more or less than an account of political legitimacy. And, at this point, I have repeated my own such account many times.

With this in mind, consider the following, from Huemer's closing statement:

> It cannot be that our right against coercion contains an exception clause whereby the right doesn't apply if coercing us would prevent more coercion by someone else. Now, Layman didn't *exactly* propose that exception (he didn't say exactly what condition he was proposing). But the exception that his view requires is *uncomfortably close* to that. There would have to be an exception built into our right against coercion whereby the right doesn't apply against the government if the government's coercing us is necessary to prevent a larger total amount of coercion. That may not be *formally inconsistent* with the notion of an agent-centered constraint, but it's completely implausible if you believe in agent-centered constraints.[1]

I propose nothing remotely like this. First of all, I'm not sure how to even make sense of a totally general right against coercion, and I certainly have not endorsed any such right. But, more importantly, I do not claim that any government, or, indeed, anyone at all, has a right to do anything because doing so will minimize instances of the same behavior. Rather – and I repeat – agents of properly

---

1. Huemer, this book, Chapter 5, Section 2, p. 174.

democratic communities have a right to coerce within the scope of their legal offices insofar as that coercion is part of an equally basically accountable legal system for determining, adjudicating, and enforcing rights. Since the minimizing rule Huemer addresses bears no significant relationship to anything I've said, I will simply move on to his next concern.

3   Anti-Exceptionalism

In my previous chapter, I suggested that Huemer's critique of legitimacy seems to turn on a principle that I named "Anti-Exceptionalism." That principle states:

> **Anti-Exceptionalism:** Condition C justifies action A when performed by the state if, and only if, C justifies A when performed by anyone at all.

I argued that Anti-Exceptionalism begs the question against the defender of state authority. For, insofar as states do have authority to do what they do, this authority must surely be exceptional. Indeed, it must be exceptional in much the same way that parental authority is exceptional. Parental authority exists, insofar as it does, in virtue of a highly exceptional relationship between a parent and child, one in which other individuals cannot stand to one another. Consequently, if we assume Anti-Exceptionalism, we thereby assume that political authority, parental authority, and other kinds of authority grounded in very special relationships cannot be genuine. But to assume this much is simply to assume from the beginning that there is no state authority. And this, of course, begs the question against my position.

Huemer is not impressed with my suggestion that he endorses Anti-Exceptionalism, and I will attempt to address his concerns. First, though, I need to answer the charges of argumentative misconduct that he has levelled against me.

First, and most obviously, I do not reject arguments by analogy. Indeed, I rely on analogical argumentation in my appeal to the example of parenthood, an example that Huemer oddly does not discuss at all. In rejecting Anti-Exceptionalism, I am not rejecting arguments that compare one thing to another. I am merely insisting that we cannot establish from the outset a standard for legitimacy that states cannot in principle meet.

Second, and almost equally obviously, I do not reject Supervenience. To the contrary, I very much agree that for a special moral relationship to exist between two people or groups, there must be a corresponding descriptive feature of their relationship that explains their special moral relationship. I disagree, however, in that I believe that there *is* a relevant descriptive difference between properly democratic governments and all other actors, albeit in virtue of a descriptive property that only such governments can possess. This property is, of course, that of defining, adjudicating, and enforcing rights subject to equal basic accountability.

With these confusions cleared away, we may productively return to the substance of Huemer's arguments. His central move in response to my concern that he begs the question with Anti-Exceptionalism is to accuse *me* of begging the question. According to him, the only reason I offer for governments' special authority is that they are (sometimes) democratic. However, as we see by way of such examples as his story about diners voting to make one person at the table pay for the whole party, other entities besides governments can also be democratic. So, unless I grant that private entities (such as the group of diners) are just as authoritative as the kind of state I have identified as authoritative, I beg the question in favor of state authority. Huemer writes:

> Layman seems to be claiming that the relevant difference between the government and private agents can be something that isn't even a difference between them – i.e., one can cite a feature that the government actually shares with some private agents, yet claim that it explains why the government gets to do things that those private agents don't get to do. This is like the theory that the reason why oranges are better than *equally sweet* grapes is that oranges are sweet . . . By the way, it's worth thinking about who is actually begging the question here . . . If you just start out saying that governments have authority partly in virtue of *being governments*, and you declare this as a brute, inexplicable fact, then of course no one could refute this.[2]

---

2. Huemer, this book, Chapter 5, Section 3, pp. 178–179.

This is a serious charge indeed. Fortunately, though, it misses its mark by a wide margin. Huemer seems to be interpreting me as claiming that governments are authoritative only when, and because, they are democratic; that is, only when, and because, their actions are subject to determination by majority vote. If this were my position, then it would indeed be improper to claim that the dinner party that votes to make one of its members pay is any less authoritative than the kinds of states to which I attribute authority. However, this is not my position at all. As I have repeated many times now, my view is that governments are authoritative to the extent that they secure equal liberty within rights by comprehensively defining, adjudicating, and enforcing rights through institutions subject to equal basic accountability. In doing so, they remedy the state of nature defects that subject people to pervasive arbitrary power and, consequently, to the vitiation of their rights.

Now, it is indeed true on my view that any entity that possess political authority must be democratic; democracy is a necessary condition of political authority. However, there can be – and, indeed, there are – many groups that are democratic but do not secure equal liberty within rights by comprehensively defining, adjudicating, and enforcing rights through institutions subject to equal basic accountability. That is why democracy is insufficient for the kind of authority that governments possess despite being necessary for such authority. So, yes; governments are special on my view. But they are not special simply because they are governments. Rather, they are special because they alone can fulfill the necessary and sufficient conditions of authority of the kind I have been discussing.

To further clarify this point, we may productively return to the example of parenthood. It is, I suppose, a necessary condition of parental authority that parents be willing to protect and educate their children, even at great cost to themselves. If someone has given birth to a child but is unwilling to do this, her parental authority is seriously in question. But this doesn't mean that any person who is willing to protect and educate a particular child at great cost to herself has parental authority over that child. If, for instance, a child has an aunt who not only meets these criteria but does so more completely than the child's mother, this does not suffice to establish that the aunt has parental authority over the child. For, under normal circumstances, parental authority also requires either biologically producing the child or, in the absence of one or more willing and able biological parents, undertaking highly specific adoption procedures. Parental authority thus turns on both a feature that many people can possess, namely willingness to provide care to the point of self-sacrifice, and a feature that only a very few people can possess, namely biologically fathering or mothering a child or, in the absence of at least one willing and able biological parent, adopting a child.

Governmental authority similarly turns on a feature that many groups can possess (being democratic) in addition to a unique feature that can be possessed only by entities that secure equal liberty within rights by comprehensively defining, adjudicating, and enforcing rights through institutions subject to equal basic accountability. To insist on the uniqueness of this later feature is in no way question-begging. Indeed, if one were to observe an entity that one was not initially inclined to think of as a government standing in this comprehensive relationship to a group of people and their rights, one would remark, "Oh! I see. It's a government after all." Thus, government authority is special, but it is not brute or inexplicable. It is special because only functioning governments (though perhaps not everything that claims to be a government) can correct the three state of nature defects by comprehensively defining, enforcing, and adjudicating rights. And, to the extent that governments do this in a way that is subject, through democracy, to equal basic accountability, they do so authoritatively.

4 Civil Disobedience

It is now time to return for the last time to the issue of civil disobedience, which has occupied a central place in the dialectic of this book. In his final chapter, Huemer raises two primary worries about my discussion of civil disobedience in my second chapter. The first of these concerns the idea of rule of law and the possibility of disrespecting it by evading the legal consequences of justified civil disobedience. The second concerns the importance of any disrespect that might (contrary to fact, in his view) be constituted by evading those consequences. Let's take them in turn.

In my second chapter, I wrote that evading the legal consequences of civil disobedience disrespects the civilly disobedient person's fellow citizens insofar as it disrespects "the whole system of rights whose definition, adjudication, and enforcement constitutes rule of law in [one's] community."[3] Huemer says that he can't understand this, because he doesn't know what rule of law is. He asks: "What is rule of law, anyway?"[4] I was sorry to hear that Huemer doesn't know what rule of law is. Happily, though, I do know what it is, and I don't mind explaining.

Rule of law is the state of affairs that exists in a community when all private and public power therein is constrained by and answerable to a system of law. Since classical times, philosophers have contrasted rule of law with the "rule of men," or, as we would now do better to put it, the rule of particular people. The basic idea is that in communities ruled by law, no one, however rich or well connected she may be, gets to make anyone else do what she wants simply because she wants it. Where law rules, the rich and well-connected are no less answerable to law's demands, and so no more able to substitute their own wills for law, than are the poor and marginalized. Thus, legal philosopher Gerald Postema writes: "Throughout its long history, the idea [of rule of law] has been rooted in the thought that the law promises protection and recourse against the arbitrary exercise of power."[5] Rule of law assumes special importance in a democratic community of the kind I have argued can be authoritative, as it is through law's rule that democratic citizens rule their community together.

Aside: Legality

Even more basic than the idea of rule of law is the idea of legality, or the character rules must have in order to count as laws at all. In his celebrated book, *The Morality of Law* (New Haven: Yale University Press, 1964), the twentieth-century legal philosopher Lon Fuller argues that in order to be genuine law, a rule must be: 1) promulgated, or publicly announced; 2) not-retroactive; 3) general, or not aimed at particular people or groups; 4) clear; 5) consistent; 6) possible to follow; 7) consistent with other state rules and actions; and 8) stable. Do you think anything is missing from this list? Why or why not?

---

3. Layman, this book, Chapter 4, Section 5, p. 161.
4. Huemer, this book, Chapter 5, Section 4, p. 180.
5. Postema 2014, p. 10.

With this much in mind, let's consider Huemer's challenge that "if you think there's some sort of obligation to respect the rule of law, then *the original disobedience* must be wrong."[6] Huemer is in error here: It does not follow that it must be wrong to disobey a particular law if there is an obligation to respect the rule of law. This would perhaps be true if, as Huemer incorrectly suggests, the rule of law amounted to "the principle that laws should always be followed."[7] But this is not what rule of law is at all. As I have explained, rule of law is the state of affairs that exists in a community when all private and public power therein is constrained by and answerable to a system of law. It is entirely possible for particular laws to be at odds with rule of law so understood; if a particular law or laws places some citizens above or below the law, it violates law's rule, and respect for law's rule may allow or even require disobedience to it. But, by the same token, a political community that includes some laws of this kind may remain a merely flawed political community rather than a failed one. Under such conditions, citizens still substantively rule together as equals through law's rule, and law's rule, which of course includes its mechanisms of enforcement, still merits the respect of those subject to it. That is how it makes sense for a person to have both a right (or even a duty) to violate a particular law and an obligation to respect the rule of law by accepting prosecution for her violation.

The ideas I have been developing here are not new. Indeed, they appear in some of the twentieth century's most important works on law and citizenship, Martin Luther King, Jr.'s "Letter from a Birmingham Jail" not least among them. King writes there of the kind of civilly disobedient activism that landed him in jail:

> I submit that an individual who breaks a law that conscience tells him is unjust, and who willingly accepts the penalty . . . in order to arouse the conscience of the community over its injustice, is in reality expressing the highest respect for law.[8]

---

6. Huemer, this book, Chapter 5, Section 4, p. 181.
7. Huemer, this book, Chapter 5, Section 4, p. 181.
8. King 1963, p. 9.

I agree with King; civil disobedience as he describes it can indeed "express the highest respect for law" in virtue of standing up for law's rule in the face of particular laws that work against that rule.

Huemer, as you have seen, denies all that I have just said about the rule of law and the possibility of objectionably disrespecting it by refusing to submit in the face of civil disobedience. But, in the second part of his final treatment of civil disobedience, he grants for the sake of argument that such refusal does constitute disrespect for rule of law in the sense (on which I earlier insisted) of a failure to value it – and, thus, others – properly. According to him even if we grant all of this, there is still no obligation to submit to law in the face of justified civil disobedience. This is because if "a bizarre terrorist group" threatened to harm you unless you disrespected something very valuable, you would be justified in engaging in the disrespect instead of submitting to the terrorists' harm.[9]

First of all, as Huemer rightly notes, it may not even make sense to think of someone in this unfortunate position as genuinely disrespecting whatever it is that the terrorists want her to disrespect, especially once we grant that the relevant sense of disrespect is not that of mere insult. To return to my previous example, a manager who fails to read reports by women because a gunman refuses to let him read them presumably does not disrespect the women who wrote the reports, even though ignoring their reports would constitute disrespect under normal circumstances. But no matter; let's suppose for a moment the coerced disrespect does make sense. Even so, the terrorist example is entirely beside the point. Huemer imagines harm being threatened by a "bizarre terrorist group" because such a group paradigmatically lacks standing to impose harm on anyone. But, as I have been arguing, merely flawed democratic governments of the kind I have endorsed do have standing to enforce their laws. The whole force of Huemer's example here turns on the assumption that governments of this sort are relevantly like terrorist groups, but the claim for which I have been arguing throughout this book is that governments of the right sort are not relevantly like terrorist groups. So, insofar as my main claim stands, it is not a problem for me that it would be okay – on the assumption that it would be possible – to disrespect others at terrorist gunpoint.

---

9. Huemer, this book, Chapter 5, Section 4, p. 181.

There is one thing I'd like to note about my position on civil disobedience before leaving the subject for the last time. Although I have argued that civilly disobedient citizens should not attempt to evade any punishments their communities impose on them for their civil disobedience, I have not argued – and I do not believe – that states normally *should* punish civilly disobedient citizens. Since civil disobedience can play a significant role in law's rule, I am inclined to think that states should generally allow special criminal defenses for civilly disobedient conduct. The Canadian philosopher Kimberley Brownlee has argued that states should recognize an exculpatory "demands of conviction" defense and a justificatory "necessity defense" for civilly disobedient citizens, and I believe that these defenses (or others like them) would likely be good policy. Nevertheless, when merely flawed democracies decide not to allow such defenses, their civilly disobedient citizens generally should not attempt to evade the legal consequences of their disobedience.[10]

5 Conclusion

During the eighteenth century, the Scottish philosopher David Hume argued that politics emerges from the human situation insofar as that situation is characterized by both scarcity of resources and limited altruism. He wrote:

> Nothing is more certain, than that men are, in a great measure, governed by interest, and that even when they extend their concern beyond themselves, it is not to any great distance; nor is it usual for them, in common life, to look farther than their nearest friends and acquaintance. It is no less certain, that it is impossible for men to consult, their interest in so effectual a manner, as by an universal and inflexible observance of the rules of justice, by which alone they can preserve society, and keep themselves from falling into that wretched and savage condition, which is commonly represented as the state of nature.[11]

---

10. Brownlee 2012, Chapters 5 & 6.
11. Hume 2000, 3.2.7 (p. 342).

On Hume's account, political community is a kind of second-best arrangement, a remedy for human beings' regrettable but predictable selfishness in the face of scarcity. If people were only less selfish, there would be no need for the state. While Hume is no doubt right that we human beings are frequently much more selfish than we aspire to be, I have argued here that our moral situation would call for government even in the absence of abiding selfishness. This is because human beings possess a high and equal moral status that, as Locke put the point fifty years earlier, demands that each person be actually able to live "without asking leave, or depending upon the will of any other man."[12] Since we are embodied social beings, we are all necessarily interdependent, and that's not a bad thing. But if that interdependence is to respect our rightful equality, it must be subject to constraint that is answerable to all of us equally. That is why democratic government can be – and sometimes is – authoritative.

Bibliography

Brownlee, Kimberley. 2012. *Conscience and Conviction: The Case for Civil Disobedience*. Oxford: Oxford University Press.

Fuller, Lon. 1964. *The Morality of Law*. New Haven: Yale University Press.

Hume, David. 2000 [1739–40]. *A Treatise of Human Nature*, ed. David Fate Norton and Mary J. Norton. New York: Oxford University Press.

King, Jr., Martin Luther. 1963. *Letter from a Birmingham Jail*. The Martin Luther King, Jr. Research and Education Institute. Stanford University (online).

Locke, John. 1988 [1689]. *Two Treatises of Government*, ed. Peter Laslett. Cambridge: Cambridge University Press.

Postema, Gerald. 2014. "Law's Rule: Reflexivity, Mutual Accountability, and the Rule of Law", in *Bentham's Theory of Law and Public Opinion*, ed. Michael Quinn and Xiaobo Zhai. Cambridge: Cambridge University Press.

---

12. Locke 1988, § 4.

Further Reading

Readings Recommended by Michael Huemer

For more about all the ideas I discussed herein, see my books *The Problem of Political Authority* and *Justice Before the Law*.

For more on the moral problems with state authority, I recommend Robert Nozick's *Anarchy, State, and Utopia*, especially the passage on "the Tale of the Slave" (pp. 290–92). Even though Nozick isn't an anarchist, this passage illuminates the intuitive moral problem with government. Lysander Spooner's *No Treason: The Constitution of No Authority* also gives a great explanation of why the U.S. Constitution has no authority.

To understand anarcho-capitalism and how it would work, see David Friedman's *The Machinery of Freedom* or Murray Rothbard's *For a New Liberty*. Friedman also gives a lot of insight into how capitalism really works, in contrast with government.

For more on the defects of democracy, see Jason Brennan's *Against Democracy*, Bryan Caplan's *The Myth of the Rational Voter*, and Christopher Achen and Larry Bartels' *Democracy for Realists*.

For more on civil disobedience, see Henry David Thoreau's classic essay "Civil Disobedience" (originally titled *Resistance to Civil Government*). There, Thoreau explains why he thought he was morally obligated to refuse to pay taxes, because his taxes would be used to help support slavery and the Mexican War.

Finally, as with most philosophical topics, the *Stanford Encyclopedia of Philosophy* is a terrific resource to learn about the current state of the discussion and the other important works to read (https://plato.stanford.edu). See especially the entries "Authority," "Political Legitimacy," "Political Obligation," and "Anarchism."

Readings Recommended by Daniel Layman

Most of the concepts on which I have relied in my chapters have their roots in just three major works from the seventeenth and eighteenth centuries: *Two Treatises of Government* by John Locke (1689), *The Social Contract* by Jean-Jacques Rousseau (1762), and *The Metaphysics of Morals* by Immanuel Kant (1797). The first two of these are widely and cheaply available in numerous good English translations. For Kant's text, see the excellent 2017 edition from Cambridge University Press, edited by Lara Denis and translated by Mary Gregor.

These early modern texts can be difficult, so it is often a good idea to work through them with a good commentary at your side. For Locke, I recommend A. John Simmons, *The Lockean Theory of Rights* (Princeton: Princeton University Press, 1992). For Rousseau, I recommend Joshua Cohen, *Rousseau: A Free Community of Equals* (New York: Oxford University Press, 2010). And, for Kant, I recommend Arthur Ripstein, *Force and Freedom: Kant's Legal and Political Philosophy* (Cambridge, Mass.: Harvard University Press, 2009).

My argument for democratic authority turns heavily on the idea of freedom from arbitrary power. This idea has its most important recent development in Philip Pettit, *On the People's Terms: A Republican Theory and Model of Democracy* (Cambridge: Cambridge University Press, 2012).

Another important concept for my argument is reasonable disagreement. For a seminal treatment of this concept that still anchors much of the academic discourse on the subject, see John Rawls, *Political Liberalism* (New York: Columbia University Press, 1993).

You've no doubt noticed (or soon will) that civil disobedience comes up in every chapter in this book. For two excellent (and challenging) recent treatments, see Kimberley Brownlee, *Conscience and Conviction: The Case for Civil Disobedience* (Oxford: Oxford University Press, 2012) and Candice Delmas, *A Duty to Resist: When Disobedience Should Be Uncivil* (New York: Oxford University Press, 2018).

Finally, although anarcho-capitalism is a recurring presence in these chapters, it is neither the only alternative to statism nor the most historically significant alternative. Over the past two centuries, most anarchists have embraced forms of left-anarchism, which is sometimes called anarcho-socialism or anarcho-syndicalism. For an important twentieth-century defense of this position, see Emma Goldman's 1911 work, *Anarchism and Other Essays*, which is widely available online.

Glossary

Accountability An agent, A, is accountable to another agent or group, B, to the extent that (1) A owes something to B; (2) B has standing to insist to A that A discharge her obligation; and (3) B can rely on institutional backup in support of her claim against A.

Ad hoc argument An argument made up after the fact to support a foregone conclusion.

Agent-centered constraint A moral principle that forbids one from mistreating others in certain ways even if doing so would prevent a larger amount of such mistreatment committed by other people. For example, one may not murder an innocent person, even to prevent someone else from murdering two innocent people.

Anarchism The view that the ideal social system would lack a government. Typically, anarchists hold that social order could be provided through non-governmental mechanisms.

Anarcho-capitalism A hypothetical social system in which the functions of protecting individual rights and adjudicating disputes would be provided by competing private businesses, rather than a government.

Arbitrary power Power governed only by the mere will of the power holder rather than by a structure of law or other binding norms.

Begging the question The fallacy one commits when one or more premises of one's argument depend for their justification on the conclusion.

Capitalism An economic system in which the means of producing goods ("capital") are controlled mainly by private individuals and organizations.

Civil disobedience The practice of disobeying a law for moral reasons, usually in the hope of causing a change in the law.

Conscientious refusal Refusal to obey an unjust law on the grounds that it is unjust.

Claim right A person is said to have a (claim) right to X provided that there is an enforceable, agent-centered constraint against depriving the person of X. A constraint is "enforceable" if it would be morally appropriate to use coercion to prevent people from violating the constraint.

Consequentialism The view that the right action is always the action with the best overall consequences, that is, one should always maximize the good.

Content independence The state's authority is said to be "content independent" provided that it does not depend on the particular commands issued by the state being objectively correct or well chosen – that is, the state may enforce laws and we have to obey them, even when they are bad laws.

Equal basic accountability A government's accountability to the entire body of its citizens through democratic mechanisms.

Executive defect (in state of nature) The absence of adequate mechanisms for enforcing rights outside of the state.

Explicit consent Consent that is communicated in words (may be either spoken or written).

Failed state A state that fails to correct the three state-of-nature defects through equally basically accountable democratic institutions to any substantial degree.

Flawed state A state that corrects, to a substantial but incomplete degree, the three state-of-nature defects through equally basically accountable democratic institutions.

Government Roughly, an organization that makes rules for the rest of society, coercively imposes those rules, and coercively maintains a monopoly on these activities.

Hypothetical consent Consent that was not actually given but would have been given under some hypothetical conditions.

Hypothetical social contract theory A theory according to which the government has authority because under certain ideal conditions, citizens *would have* agreed to establish a government and would have agreed to obey that government in exchange for the government's protection.

Implicit consent Consent that is communicated through one's actions but not explicitly in words.

Invasion (of rights)   Rights violation constituted by active interference in a person's rights.

Judicial defect (in state of nature)   The absence of adequate mechanisms for adjudicating rights outside of the state.

Jury nullification   The practice in which a jury votes to acquit a defendant, despite adequate evidence of guilt, because the jury believes that a conviction would result in injustice (may be because the law itself is unjust, or the prescribed punishment is unjustly harsh, or this defendant has extenuating circumstances).

Legislative defect (in state of nature)   The absence of adequate mechanisms for defining rights outside of the state.

Lockean Proviso   The moral requirement that people who claim previously unowned natural resources leave "enough and as good" for others.

Monopoly   A person or organization is said to "have a monopoly on" a particular product when that person or organization is the only available provider of the product.

Particularity (of political authority)   The limitation of a state's authority to the particular people who live within it or are otherwise subject to it.

Permission right   The absence of a duty to refrain from doing something.

Philosophical anarchism   The view that no actual government has political authority. Compare: political anarchism.

Political anarchism   The view that the ideal social system would lack a government. Typically, anarchists hold that social order could be provided through nongovernmental mechanisms.

Political authority   A government is said to have political authority when it has political legitimacy and the citizens have political obligations.

Political legitimacy   A content-independent entitlement on the part of the government to make and enforce commands, even in many circumstances in which it would be wrong for anyone else to make or enforce similar commands.

Political obligation   A content-independent obligation on the part of citizens to obey governmental commands *because* they come from the government.

Property rights   Claim rights over goods or services.

Reasonable disagreement   Disagreement among democratic citizens that falls within the scope of basic respect for one another and for rule of law.

Right *See* claim right; permission right; property rights.

Rule of law The state of affairs that exists in a community when all private and public power therein is constrained by and answerable to a system of law.

Self-government rights A person's claim rights to her own body and mind.

Social contract theory A theory according to which the government has authority because we have all *agreed* to obey the government in exchange for the government's protection.

State of nature A condition in which people live together without any government.

Supervenience The principle that there cannot be a moral difference between two things without some descriptive difference between them that explains the moral difference. Moral properties are said to "supervene on" descriptive properties.

Utilitarianism A form of consequentialism that holds that the right action is always the action that produces the greatest total amount of pleasure or desire-satisfaction for all beings concerned.

Vitiation (of rights) Rights violation constituted by arbitrary power to invade rights.

Index